WARNING

Changes in draft regulation or practices may make some of the information in this *Handbook* inaccurate. Keep in touch with a draft counselor near you. The nearest CCCO office can help you find one. If you are not already on CCCO's mailing list, cut out this page and return it to the nearest CCCO office. Please allow several weeks for processing. You will receive *CCCO News Notes,* published four times yearly. *News Notes* reports important changes in the draft, court cases, and other news of interest to people facing the draft. It is free of charge, but CCCO needs your contributions to continue its work.

NAME ....

ADDRESS ....

CITY ....................STATE....ZIP........

HANDBOOK FOR CONSCIENTIOUS OBJECTORS

by Robert A. Seeley
Illustrations by Karen Saler

Central Committee for Conscientious Objectors

Philadelphia   San Francisco

July, 1982

Library of Congress catalog number: 56-2629
Printed in the United States of America.
Copyright © 1981 by the Central Committee for Conscientious Objectors. All rights reserved.
ISBN 0-933368-03-8
Cover design by Daniel McClain.

First Edition, November, 1952 — 8,000 copies
Second Edition, September, 1954 — 5,000 copies
Third Edition, July, 1957 — 5,000 copies
Fourth Edition, January, 1960 — 7,000 copies
Fifth Edition, February, 1962 — 8,000 copies
Sixth Edition, April, 1964 — 2,000 copies
Seventh Edition, April, 1965 — 8,000 copies
Eighth Edition, November, 1965 — 11,000 copies
2nd Printing, March, 1966 — 15,000 copies
3rd Printing, December, 1966 — 27,000 copies
Ninth Edition, November, 1967 — 16,000 copies
2nd Printing, March, 1968 — 15,000 copies
3rd Printing, May, 1968 — 11,000 copies
4th Printing, June, 1968 — 11,000 copies
Tenth Edition, October, 1968 — 50,000 copies
2nd Printing, December, 1969 — 20,000 copies
3rd Printing, March, 1970 — 20,000 copies
4th Printing, May, 1970 — 10,000 copies
5th Printing, July, 1970 — 15,000 copies
Eleventh Edition, September, 1970 — 48,000 copies
2nd Printing, March, 1971 — 50,000 copies
3rd Printing, October, 1971 — 8,500 copies
Twelfth Edition, April, 1972 — 50,000 copies
Thirteenth Edition, April, 1981 — 10,000 copies
Second Printing, July, 1982 — 10,000 copies

Central Committee for Conscientious Objectors
2208 South Street
Philadelphia, Pennsylvania 19146

1251 Second Avenue
San Francisco, California 94122

For the victims of war

PREFACE

For twenty years, from 1952 to 1972, the *Handbook for Conscientious Objectors* was the most reliable book on conscientious objection under the U.S. draft law. When inductions ended in December, 1972, the *Handbook* stopped publication. No new edition has been published until now.

The need for a new *Handbook* became clear when the President ordered draft registration in mid-1980. Responding to the threat of a new draft, thousands of young people contacted CCCO. They wanted information on conscientious objection, and they wanted to know what they could do to protect themselves if the draft should be revived. Over 25,000 of them registered with CCCO as conscientious objectors.

At the same time, because objection to war and the military had gotten little publicity, public knowledge about conscientious objection was at its lowest point since the 1950s. CCCO counselors talked with many young people who had never heard of conscientious objection, yet were strongly against war. Some had joined the military or had thought about enlisting during the 1970s, when it was "peacetime." People wanted, and needed, to know more about war and how it affected them.

The result is this book. It is not simply an update of

earlier *Handbooks*. In the 1950s and 1960s, most people who read the *Handbook* were looking primarily for information about the draft law and how to make a CO claim under it. Readers still need and want this information, but now they need more. They need a book which talks about conscientious objection and war resistance, not as a legal problem, but as a moral problem.

To meet this need, I have written chapters on subjects like the nature of war, nuclear war, and the use of force. In addition, because the draft has been inactive, I have written a chapter which tries to put the draft into the context of military recruitment and strategy as a whole. The CCCO staff has reviewed these chapters, but I am responsible for what is said in them.

The draft regulations and other procedures have, of course, changed much since 1972. This edition of the *Handbook* takes these changes into account. A reader who decides that he or she is not a conscientious objector as the law defines it can still find much helpful information in the chapters on the draft.

There is another change from earlier editions of the *Handbook*, resulting from my experience at CCCO. In counseling people on draft and military law, I have seen that there are many different kinds of objection to war. I have learned that one kind of objection is not "better" than another—that most resisters agree on most points where war is concerned. The person who objected to the war in Vietnam but not to other wars usually objected to the same things I do; I just apply my objections to more wars.

War resisters—a term I use because I can't think of a better one—are all part of the same effort. That is true whether they apply for conscientious objector status under the draft or join the military and refuse to work with nuclear weapons. They all see that war involves moral, not just political, choice. And they have all chosen, in their ways, to say no.

Earlier *Handbooks* were directed more toward COs who qualified under the draft than is this one. My own understanding of what war resistance is is one reason. Another is my feeling that a book like this one should help people to take the stands which they can take—even if they do not fit under the narrow provisions of the draft law. If this book helps readers to see what they themselves believe, and then to act on their convictions, it will succeed.

I would be glad if every reader decided to object to all war. That happens to be my position, and it is always nice when people agree with one's views. But I know that war is a complicated issue. Reasonable people can and do disagree about it. What is most important, I think, is that readers look at war without panic or hysteria; that they break through the myths which most people believe about war; and that they decide for themselves what to do about it. I have faith that if everyone did this, we would be on our way to a more peaceful world.

I have tried to write this new *Handbook* in the simplest language I could use to convey the ideas in each chapter. This has not always been easy, because conscientious objection is a complex business. I hope, though, that readers will find this *Handbook* easier going than, say, the Selective Service regulations.

The book is addressed to the reader ("you") because, unlike previous *Handbooks*, it is relevant to women as well as men. I don't like using "he or she" over and over again, and I can't in good conscience use "he/she." Talking to the reader as "you" avoids this without, I hope, offending either sex.

Finally, I must thank the many people who have made this *Handbook* possible. I owe more than I can say to previous *Handbook* authors and editors Caleb Foote, Lyle Tatum, George Willoughby, and especially Arlo Tatum, a valued colleague and friend. My wife, Ruth Seeley, spent many hours listening, criticizing, and reacting as I formulated the ideas in Part III. The support and encouragement of the CCCO staff were essential. At great inconvenience to themselves, they voted to release me from office duties so that I could work full-time on this project. Comments on many of the chapters, especially those by Jon Landau, Bruce Jugan, Bill Galvin, and John Judge, were extensive, useful, and challenging. Larry Spears took sole responsibility for preparing *CCCO News Notes* in my absence. Eric Corson of Prisoner Visitation and Support corrected the many errors in the original manuscript of the chapter on prisons. Michael Barba raised badly needed funds to cover the cost of preparing and publishing the book. Karen Saler and Larry Sene did a splendid job on the illustrations.

Robert A. Seeley

March, 1981

WHAT'S YOUR QUESTION?

What are the draft registration rules?......Chapter 4
How would the draft work if it came back?..Chapter 3
What is a conscientious objector? ....Chapter 5
What is "religious training and belief"? ...Chapter 5
What if I don't object to all wars? ....Chapter 6
How can I begin working on my CO claim?..Chapter 7
What do COs do as alternative service? ....Chapter 8
How can I decide whether I'm against all war?
........Chapter 6, Part III
Do I have to object to all force?...........Chapter 11
What might happen in a nuclear war?.....Chapter 10
What is "total war"?....................Chapter 9
What about past and future wars? .Chapters 12 and 13
What happens if I resist the draft? .Chapter 4, Part IV
What do noncombatant soldiers do? ......Chapter 16

PROTECT YOURSELF.
FOLLOW THESE SUGGESTED RULES.

Whether or not inductions are taking place as you read this, you need to take steps to protect your rights. This is especially true if you're seeking conscientious objector status or have decided not to register for the draft. But it's also true if you're seeking another classification, like hardship deferment. By following the suggestions below, you'll increase your chances of getting the classification you seek, or of having your claim recognized in court.

•*Keep copies* of everything you send to Selective Service, either to your local board or to national Selective Service. Keep copies of everything you receive from Selective Service.

•*Make all requests, appeals, etc., in writing.* Send letters to Selective Service by certified mail, return receipt requested. Staple the receipt to your copy of the letter.

•*Do not rely on promises from local board clerks or members, or from other draft officials.* Unless you object to doing so, follow the printed instructions on all forms. If you don't understand the instructions, get help from CCCO or a draft counselor. If you talk with a draft official on the telephone, get the official's name and write a letter to Selective Service confirming in writing what you were told on the phone.

• *Present as full a case as possible* to your local board, even if you think it is hostile and will disregard everything you say. Your local board may turn out to be more fair than you thought, or, if not, having your full case on record can help you on appeal or in court.

• *Follow deadlines.* Your requests for new classifications or appeals must meet strict deadlines —usually ten days from the date your induction order or most recent classification was *mailed* to you (not the date you receive it). You must *postmark* your reply by the deadline or risk losing your appeal or chance for a different classification. If you're in doubt about what a letter from Selective Service means, appeal it. You can simply write the date, your signature, and the words "I request an appeal" on a sheet of paper and send it to Selective Service.

• *If you're away from home,* arrange for someone to look at your mail and contact you at once if you receive any notice from Selective Service. If you're abroad, leave behind a signed request for an appeal for your mail-opener to date and forward if needed.

• *Know what you believe.* If you're a conscientious objector, practice expressing your beliefs orally and in writing. If you're a church member, know where your church stands on war. This *Handbook* and the suggestions under "Further Reading" will help you to decide what you believe.

• *Keep in touch with changes in regulations.* Draft rules change. Although most of this *Handbook* probably won't be affected by these changes, the material in Chapters 2 and 3 can get out of date quickly. Don't rely on this *Handbook* alone. Get in touch with CCCO or your draft counselor for the most up-to-date information.

- *When in doubt, get help.* CCCO can help you to find a draft counselor or an attorney if you need one.

CONTENTS

Preface i
What's Your Question? v
Protect Yourself. Follow These
   Suggested Rules vii

Part I: The Draft, The Military, and You
   Chapter 1: This Handbook and You 1
   Chapter 2: The Draft and the Military 7
   Chapter 3: You and the Draft 17

Part II: War Resistance and the Law
   Chapter 4: Registration and Resistance 41
   Chapter 5: Conscientious Objection
     Under the Law 53
   Chapter 6: Selective Objection 63
   Chapter 7: Documenting Your CO Claim 71
   Chapter 8: Alternative Service 85

Part III: Thinking About War Resistance
   A Note to the Reader 93
   Chapter 9: Some Thoughts on War 95
   Chapter 10: You and Nuclear War 113
   Chapter 11: Force, Violence, and War 121
   Chapter 12: Hitler 129
   Chapter 13: If the Country Were Attacked 143

Part IV: COs in Court and Prison
   Chapter 14: COs and the Courts 153
   Chapter 15: COs in Prison 171

Part V: The Unarmed Soldier
Chapter 16: The Unarmed Soldier 181
Appendices
Questions Asked COs......................189
Further Reading 193
Some Groups Working for Peace 203
Notes on Sources............................205
Index 215

PART I

THE DRAFT, THE MILITARY, AND YOU

CHAPTER 1
THIS HANDBOOK AND YOU

On March 12, 295, in the town of Thevesta, North Africa, the conscript Maximilianus was tried by a Roman court. He had refused to take the oath as a soldier. The court sentenced him to death.*

Maximilianus, an early Christian, was probably not the first war resister. Just as we do not know when war began, so we do not know when people began to resist it. But, throughout history, hundreds of thousands, perhaps millions, have refused in one way or another to take part in war.

Some resisters, like Maximilianus, have opposed all wars. Others have opposed only the war they were asked to fight in. Still others have refused to follow orders which they thought were wrong. And many have resisted without filling out a form or telling anyone what they were doing. They simply did not register for the draft or, if they were soldiers, went absent without leave. In some units in World War II, up to three-quarters of the soldiers did not even fire their weapons at the enemy.

These people had one thing in common. All felt that war or some part of war was evil. All believed

---

*Footnotes will be found under "Notes on Sources," p. 240.

this so strongly that they could not do what they felt was wrong. Each resister, soldier or civilian, man or woman, drew a different line. But all, by their actions, said, "I cannot do this because it is wrong."

This book is about the lines which you will have to draw as a person who may face the draft and as a citizen.

War Resistance Today

War resisters today are not executed. Many countries, including the United States, have laws which recognize conscientious objection to war. But few countries provide for all kinds of war resisters. Greece, for instance, allows COs to serve as noncombatants in the military, but does not provide for civilian alternative service. And no country allows its soldiers to refuse to follow legal orders.

The law in the United States recognizes only objection to all wars. But this isn't as simple as it sounds. If you are wondering whether you qualify as an objector to all wars, you can get help from Chapters 5 and 6 and Part III of this *Handbook*.

U.S. law also recognizes only "religious" objection to war. But it defines "religious" beliefs to include moral and philosophical objection. For more information on the meaning of "religion," read Chapter 5.

Still, even though our law allows many grounds for conscientious objection, it permits only one kind of objector: the person who can't take part in any war. Do you fit in this category? Should you apply for conscientious objector status? Should you even register for the draft? What if you don't object to all wars? What can you do?

Only you can decide what you object to and what

you can accept.

But Why Think About It Now?

If you're facing the draft, you probably don't need much argument on why you should think about war. Even though you may never be drafted, the draft makes you think about where you stand because you have to.

But, like all things connected with war and peace, it isn't always that simple. The draft system may not actually be drafting anybody, or you may not be old enough to be drafted. Why worry about it now?

One answer is that you won't have much time to decide if you ever are drafted. Chapter 3 of this *Handbook* explains how the draft might work. You'll notice that you might have as little as ten days to make up your mind whether or not you're a conscientious objector. That's not much time. You wouldn't want to have to decide whether to get married in such a short time. And deciding about war is just that hard. Your decision can change your life, for better or worse. It might even lead you to resist the draft and risk a prison term.

That's why you should try to decide now, while you have more time.

There's another reason to think about war and peace. No matter where you come out on these issues, you are going to be a citizen of this country and the world. You'll probably vote in the future. And, when nuclear war could wipe out civilization, your vote will be important not just for the country, but for everyone in the world. If you decide now where you stand on war, your vote will mean that much more. And if you want to make a more peaceful world, you can do it best by knowing where you stand and why.

If You're Black or Hispanic

War is no respecter of race. In the First World War, most of those killed were white Europeans. Millions of Japanese died in World War II. And an "enemy" can become a "friend" very quickly, depending on the world situation—just as Germany and Japan did after World War II.

But it's also true that the wars since World War II have taken place mainly in the Third World. In Korea and Vietnam, U.S. troops fought against non-white peoples. France fought non-white peoples in Algeria and Indochina. And the Soviet Union invaded a Third World country when it sent troops into Afghanistan.

The U.S. military draws many recruits from the unemployed. And a great many unemployed are black and Hispanic. In the military itself, black and Hispanic people have less opportunity than whites, and most officers are whites. Some of this is caused by racism, and some by the military structure.

The whole question of war, racism, and the military is very complex. This book doesn't try to deal with it. You can get more information about it from CCCO or from some of the books listed under "Further Reading" at the end of this *Handbook*. You may find that you're opposed to the military because it discriminates. Or you may decide, as many black and Hispanic people have, that the military discriminates less than the rest of society.

No matter where you come out on these issues, though, you still need to decide where you stand on war. Do you think wars against Third World countries are wrong? Or do you oppose any wars? Do you think the many wars against Third World countries in the last thirty years are an accident? Or are they, too, a result of the war system? And what does this mean for you and your life? You are the only one who can decide.

What About Women?

Women are not now covered by the draft law. They don't have to register, and they can't be drafted. But Congress or the courts could very quickly change the law to make it cover women.

You can't rely on the fact that you're a woman Many people think women should be drafted. And if you're not drafted, you'll almost certainly get calls and letters from military recruiters. So you, too, have to decide how you feel about the military.

Women in the military have many problems—discrimination, sexual harassment, rape, among others. This book doesn't talk about them even though they are important. What it talks about is war. And that's an issue you would face even if the military were the perfect place for women.

How To Use This Book

No book is a substitute for good draft counseling. If you're confused about anything—the draft law or your own beliefs, for instance—you need to talk to someone who knows about conscientious objection and the law. CCCO can help you find good counseling. And it's best to have counseling even if you're not confused.

But you can use this *Handbook* to do two things: to learn about war and decide where you stand; and to decide how to act on your stand once you've made it.

Part I of this *Handbook* explains how the draft fits in with the rest of the U.S. military and military recruitment. It also tells how the draft is supposed to work.

6—*This Handbook and You*

Part II explains the law on conscientious objection and war resistance. In order to decide where you stand, you need to know what the choices are. You can learn about some of them from this section.

In Part III, you'll find chapters on some of the issues you might want to think about as you decide what to do. You probably won't agree with everything in these chapters, and that's good. Your opinion, not what's in this book, is what counts. These chapters are the author's opinion, not CCCO policy. They're designed to start you thinking—no matter where you finally come out.

Parts IV and V tell what happens to conscientious objectors in court and prison, and what some COs do in the military.

The section called "Further Reading" is designed to help you follow up on questions that you have or issues that interest you. You'll also find some frequently-asked questions listed under "Questions Asked COs.' And, of course, you can always get more information from CCCO.

Good luck.

CHAPTER 2
THE DRAFT AND THE MILITARY

The United States military is among the most powerful on earth. It has 2.1 million soldiers, more than any country but China and the Soviet Union. Its weapons range from rifles and tanks to nerve gas and guided missiles. It has bases, with large numbers of troops, in Europe and Asia, and may soon have a base in the Middle East. Its nuclear submarines, each armed with missiles than can destroy many cities, cruise the oceans at all times. Some of its bombers cruise the air at all times. If it released all of its nuclear weapons, it could destroy the entire human race twelve times over—or perhaps more.

To maintain its troop strength, the military must recruit 400,000 new soldiers each year. From 1948 through 1972, it used a combination of the draft and voluntary recruitment. Since 1972, it has recruited without the draft. But the draft remains on "standby" and could again become an important part of the recruitment system.

The Uses of the Military

Following World War II, the name of the War Department was changed to "Defense Department." Despite this name change, very little of the Defense budget actually goes for the defense of the United States. Much is spent on troops stationed around the world, on waste, and on weapons systems that have no military value.

From a military point of view, the United States could be defended by a much smaller Army, Navy, and Air Force than it now has. It has northern and southern borders with friendly countries, and those borders have each been unarmed for over a hundred years. On the east and west, it is bordered by oceans. An attack over water on the continental U.S., as you'll see in Chapter 13, would be so difficult that no general would try it. And in order to destroy almost any enemy, the U.S. would need to use only a small part of its nuclear arsenal.

Why, then, is the U.S. military as large as it is? The answer lies partly in American politics, where candidates can win votes by being for a "strong defense." It also lies partly in the doctrine of "deterrence," which says that the way to prevent an attack is to have so many weapons that your opponent will think the attack won't be worth the cost. For more on "deterrence," see Chapter 10.

But politics and "deterrence" alone don't explain why this country has such a large military. Since World War II ended, this country has used military force or the threat of military force over 200 times. What was this supposed to do?

One reason why the U.S. keeps so many troops when there is no war is "geopolitics." This is the contest among the countries of the world—mainly between the U.S. and the Soviet Union—for power and influence. Many in Washington and Moscow, in fact, believe that the struggle between East and West is the most important factor in world politics.

So each side tries to gain influence in other

countries, or power over them, using economic aid, military aid, persuasion—and military force. If, for instance, one side thinks that a friendly government is going to be overthrown, it may send military aid or even troops to help that government. It may even, as the U.S. did in Vietnam and the Soviet Union did in Afghanistan, install a government of its own choice to replace the one that is weak. "Geopolitics" often leads to military intervention. In fact, since World War II, the U.S. has fought wars of intervention in Korea and Vietnam.

But "geopolitics" doesn't always lead to a shooting war. Since World War II, the U.S. has signed treaties agreeing that it will defend many countries. The most famous of these is the North Atlantic Treaty Organization, or NATO, which is supposed to prevent the Soviet Union from conquering Europe. The Soviet Union, in its turn, has signed a treaty, called the Warsaw Pact, with the communist governments of Eastern Europe. One purpose of the Warsaw Pact is to "balance" NATO—to keep NATO from conquering Eastern Europe. NATO also seeks to "balance" the Warsaw Pact. Each side does this by deploying troops and weapons systems. And when one side deploys a new system, the other is almost sure to follow suit. This is "geopolitics" without a shot fired. You'll have to decide for yourself whether it makes war more or less likely.

Outside of Europe, the U.S., the Soviet Union, and other Western countries compete in the Third World, not just for influence, but for natural resources. You've heard a great deal about the Middle East and oil, but the Third World provides other resources as well. Many important metals, like chromium, are no longer found in the U.S. U.S. troops are sometimes used to protect U.S. "interests" in countries that have natural resources. This doesn't always mean intervention. It could mean sending an aircraft carrier to a region to restore "stability." The Soviet Union protects its own "interests," too, by helping friendly governments. As both countries use up their own resources, the competition between them may become more intense than it is now.

At the same time, many Third World countries are saying that they have the right to decide for themselves what they will do with their natural resources. Unpopular governments are often overthrown by guerilla movements. Many of these governments were friendly to the U.S. This could lead to more wars of intervention. It could change the balance of power in the world. Or it could do both.

Maintaining all these uses of the military takes millions of troops, billions of dollars worth of weapons, and hundreds of billions of dollars in tax money each year.

Recruiting the Military

Tens of thousands of troops leave the military each year. Some leave because their time is up. Others get early discharges because they are not doing well in the military, because of family problems, or for other reasons. To replace those who leave, the military recruits 400,000 new troops each year.

Military recruitment today relies on a combination of high unemployment among young people, advertising campaigns, and promises of education and job training. Pentagon figures show that as unemployment among young people rises, military recruitment also goes up. The military spends tens of millions of dollars on advertising each year. And recruiters persuade many people to come into the military by telling them about special programs like electronics school and promising them education and training in a field they choose.

For many recruits, the promise of education and training quickly turn to disappointment. Military enlistment agreements allow the military to keep a recruit even when the military doesn't fulfill its promises. And the needs of the military are more important to military planners than providing education for a new recruit. A recruit who was promised training in auto mechanics may get the training he or she was promised—and then be assigned to work in artillery.

In addition, much military training teaches skills that are no use in civilian life. A person experienced in artillery, for instance, isn't likely to find civilian work in that field. Artillery is used only in the military.

Minority soldiers and women often find that they're no more equal in the military than they would be in civilian life—sometimes less. In the military as a whole, less than 2% of officers are black, while over 10% of enlisted people are black. And women often end up stuck in traditional "women's jobs," like typing.

It's not surprising that many people want to leave the military early or don't want to re-enlist when their hitches are up.

The Draft and Recruitment

In many of the years since inductions ended, military recruiters have not signed up all the recruits they were supposed to. Called a "shortfall," this lack of new recruits has led to calls for a new draft. Some people have supported the draft all along, even when it wasn't in use.

It's true that when the draft was active there were no shortfalls. Induction quotas were based on the expected shortfall, and draftees made up the gap between the number of people who enlisted and the number of people the military wanted. The draft also put pressure on many people who might not have enlisted. In order to avoid being drafted into the Army, these people would join up with the Navy, Air Force, or Marines. Or they might join a Reserve unit.

So the draft made military recruiting easier. But it also, according to some critics, made for inefficient use of troops. Military personnel were sometimes used where civilian employees could have been—for instance, in providing food service at military bases in the U.S. And Congress members looking for military waste found that soldiers were mowing lawns for generals and fixing officers' private cars for free.

It's important to keep this in mind when you're thinking about or discussing the draft and the all-volunteer military. Another point to keep in mind is that the U.S. military has never been a "draft military" in the sense that most soldiers were draftees. Even at the height of the Vietnam draft, for instance, only about 500,000 out of 3 million U.S. troops were drafted. The rest enlisted. And many of them would have enlisted, draft or no draft.

Many of these "true volunteers," as the military calls them, joined up because they could not find work. Or because they wanted education—just like today. So it's not true that a "fair" draft (if there is any such thing) would spread around the burdens of serving in the military. A lot of people would still enlist because they were poor and desperate for jobs. At least that would be true unless the military refused to take any volunteers. That's not very likely.

The Standby Draft

The Military Selective Service Act, as revised in 1971, says that if inductions end, the draft system is to remain in "standby" status. When the law was written, many in Congress thought this meant that people would be registered, classified, and perhaps even given physical examinations. It hasn't worked out that way. From 1972 to 1974, people were required to register, and local boards did actually classify them. Registration was suspended in 1975, but a new registration was proclaimed in July, 1980.

The idea behind the standby draft is to keep a "pool" of possible draftees ready for an emergency. But it's not clear what would be an "emergency," or whether such a crisis is likely.

Most people in Congress and the Pentagon talk about being ready for an attack by the Warsaw Pact in Europe. And there's no doubt that, because of the large armies stationed there, Europe looks pretty tense at times. But many experts believe that war is less likely in Europe than in other places, like the Middle East. They also think that a large war in Europe would be a nuclear war, and large armies wouldn't be very useful in such a war. It's hard to know. What we do know—because Pentagon spokespersons told the press about it—is that in the last "mobilization exercise" which the Defense Department held, the mock mobilization was for a European war.

So, even though you may not think a war in Europe is going to happen, the Pentagon and Congress think it's important to plan for one. That's one reason why they want a standby draft and draft registration. It may also be the reason given for reviving inductions —not that there is such a war, but that there may be.

The Uses of the Draft

But, in fact, since World War II, there has been no war on the continent of Europe. And the draft has been used for two wars: Korea and Vietnam. The draft could be used for these wars and others like them because it makes expanding the military very easy. If more troops are needed, they can be drafted. That's true even if the war they're being used for is unpopular. There's little doubt that the draft made the Vietnam War easier to prolong because it supplied troops who wouldn't otherwise have gone.

Conscription (another name for the draft) also changes military strategy. At least it has in earlier wars. If a general can simply draft more troops, he's less likely to worry about having a lot of them killed and wounded. Napoleon, who had the first modern draft, once boasted that he could afford to lose 25,000 soldiers a month—a very large number of casualties for that time. Generals on both sides in World War I fought a "war of attrition" in which they were willing to accept tens of thousands of casualties each month, as long as the other side lost more. They couldn't have done this without conscription. And in Vietnam, the U.S. generals often said that they could win the war if only they had more troops. This may or may not have been true, but it would almost surely have led to more Americans being killed.

Your Decision

Many people are against the standby draft and refuse to go along with it. These resisters often object not only to war, but to the idea of conscription itself. In addition to making war easier and more deadly, they say, the draft interferes with peoples' lives and their rights.

You'll have to decide for yourself whether you agree with this—and whether you'll go along with draft registration if you should face it. Before you can decide on this, though, you need to know more about the draft and war. That's what the rest of this book is about.

CHAPTER 3
YOU AND THE DRAFT

Inductions under the draft ended in 1972. Since then, the draft has been on "standby" or "deep standby" status. Men born in 1960 and 1961 were required to register in January, 1981. They are now required to register as they turn 18. But, since 1974, no one has been classified (except in Class 1-H) or given an Armed Forces physical examination. The President's power to order inductions into the military expired in 1973.

The end of inductions, though, hasn't meant the end of the draft—on paper. Except for the President's power to induct, the draft law is still on the books. And while the draft has been on standby, Selective Service officials have changed the draft rules to make the system more efficient. They've also made it necessary for you to act fast if there are new inductions in the future.

Nobody knows what the draft will really be like if inductions are reinstated. This chapter is based on the draft law itself (the Military Selective Service Act) and on Selective Service regulations which were made final in February, 1982. But much of what's in this chapter could change before there are new inductions. Congress might rewrite the draft law. Selective Service might rewrite the regulations. More important, nobody has ever seen the new rules in practice.

So this chapter is only a good guess how the draft might work. Don't rely on it. Talk to a draft counselor.

Induction Authority

You'll probably have at least some warning before inductions begin again. This is because the President can't just order new inductions. Congress not only has to approve the needed money; they have to extend the President's power to induct. Even in an emergency that would take a day or two. If the draft were brought back to fill recruiter shortfalls, it could take months.

The President's power to induct in the past has covered only inductions into the active military, mainly the Army. There's no guarantee that this will happen in the future. Some in Congress want to set up a draft for the Reserves. Some want to make the inductions authority permanent. Others want to create a universal draft for the military and for civilian public works ("national service"). Still others oppose any draft at all. In an emergency, the draft would probably be reinstated quickly. But you can see that a proposal for a new peacetime draft would lead to a long debate.

You can't, however, rely on having warning. It's best to prepare yourself now. As you'll see below, the draft regulations don't give you much time to make a claim for deferment, exemption, or conscientious objector status.

The Structure of the Draft

On paper, the Selective Service System has many parts. Most of them are not operating right now, but would if inductions began again. Some of them, like the Computer Service Center, may not be legal. At least they're not part of the draft law itself. This section—like the rest of this chapter—ignores questions like whether the new draft rules are legal or fair. It's a description only—not a guess at how the courts may rule in the future.

At the top of the Selective Service System is the Director of Selective Service. He or she has headquarters in Washington and is responsible for administering the draft system. The Director also has the power to grant "administrative classifications" like 4-A (veteran) which involve no judgment. This power would be delegated to Selective Service Area Offices if inductions began again.

Not mentioned in the draft Act is the Computer Service Center, located in Great Lakes, Illinois. This is Selective Service's computer system—like a giant mailing list. Stored in the draft system's computers is the Registrant Information Bank (RIB), which contains data on men who have registered for the draft since the RIB was set up in the mid-1970s. If you registered during 1980 or 1981, you're now part of the RIB. The Computer Service Center would issue classification cards and induction orders if inductions began again.

There is one State Director of Selective Service for each state, plus State Directors for New York City, Guam, Puerto Rico, the Virgin Islands, and the District of Columbia. The State Director's powers were not clear as this *Handbook* went to press. State Directors have been appointed on a "standby" basis.

There are five Regional Offices of Selective Service. Each of these Regional Offices is responsible for the several states in its region. The law doesn't provide for Regional Offices.

Area Offices operate within a state and administer several local boards. For instance, there might be an Area Office for Philadelphia to run all the Philadelphia local boards.

Regional Offices are now running; Area Offices are not.

In order to decide "judgmental classifications" like applications for conscientious objector status, Selective Service would have three levels of "claims boards." Local Boards, which must have at least three members, would be responsible for a county, a part of a county, or (in special cases) several counties together. Your local board would be the first to look at your application for a "judgmental classification."

Above your Local Board would be a District Appeal Board. There would be one such Appeal Board for each Federal judicial district, so many states would actually have more than one Appeal Board. Appeal Boards are often divided into panels to handle their workload more promptly. Above the District Appeal Board would be the National Selective Service Appeal Board. This last board would hear appeals "to The President" and would be appointed directly by the President.

Selective Service recently appointed 10,000 local board members and has now set up just over 2,000 local boards.

Registration

If you're required to register, the first step in the draft procedures would be registration. At present the law covers only men, but Congress could add women before new inductions could take place. For details on registration and resistance to registration, see the next chapter.

To make things simpler, let's assume that you've decided to register for the draft and apply for conscientious objector status.

There is no chance for you to make your CO application at registration. You can follow some of the suggestions in the next chapter, but if you don't try to apply for CO status at registration, you won't hurt your case. All that happens at registration is that your name and address are placed on the draft system's computers. The Registration Card (SSS Form 3) says that you're required to give your Social Security Number as well. If you don't want to give the draft system your Social Security Number, consult your draft counselor or CCCO before you take any action.

Once your name is in the computer, and Selective Service has checked to see that they have your correct address, you would simply be kept in Class 1-H (holding classification) until registrants (people who have registered for the draft) of your year are being called for induction. Nothing would happen until you were assigned a Random Sequence Number (RSN), often called a lottery number. You can use this time to prepare your CO claim, gather references, etc. And you should because once things *do* begin to happen, they'll happen very fast.

The Lottery

If inductions were reinstated tomorrow, all men who had registered would probably receive their lottery numbers in a single drawing. After the first drawing, however, you would probably receive your lottery number in the year you turn 19. For example, if you were born in 1965, and inductions had been reinstated in 1982, you would be required to register in 1983 and would be assigned your lottery number in 1984. There would be a new lottery drawing each year.

Lottery numbers would be based on your date of

birth. For example, May 1 might be assigned RSN 256, May 2 RSN 37, and so on. There's no way to predict your lottery number. The date of birth which Selective Service would use would be the one you last gave them—probably the one you listed when you registered. If for some reason they have an incorrect date of birth for you, consult your draft counselor about what to do. Once you've been assigned a lottery number, Selective Service will not change it even if you give them a new date of birth. But it's not clear whether the rule that requires this is legal.

Uniform National Call

In the year in which you turn 20, you would enter the "age 20 selection group" for induction. This would include all registrants born in your year of birth.

Selective Service's Uniform National Call would be based on the number of draftees which the Pentagon requested during a given time period. This in turn would be based on the predicted shortfall, just as it was under previous drafts. Under the Uniform National Call, the Director of Selective Service would establish an "induction cutoff" number. For simplicity, let's suppose the cutoff was 100 and your lottery number was 27. (If the first cutoff didn't "produce" enough draftees, a second a higher cutoff would be set, and so on until the draft system's quota was filled.)

All registrants whose numbers were 100 or less would be classified 1-A. You would first learn of your 1-A classification when you received your induction order.

If your lottery number was not reached at all during your "selection" year, you would drop into the "age

21 selection group" and would only be called when all registrants in the next year's age 20 selection group had been called. Since this isn't very likely, in practice you'd probably only be "exposed" to possible induction for a year.

Order of Call

Selective Service would call up registrants for induction in the following order:

• Volunteers for induction, in the order they volunteered.

• Registrants who had postponements of induction, but whose postponements have expired.

• Registrants in the age 20 selection group for the current year who have received deferments or exemptions which have now expired. These people would be called up in order of lottery numbers. All of them would have received induction orders before they applied for deferment or exemption.

• Registrants in the age 20 selection group who have not already received induction orders, in order of lottery numbers.

• Registrants in previous selection groups, like the age 21 selection group. The age 21 selection group, then the age 22 selection group, and so on until Selective Service reached the age 25 selection group. Within each selection group, people would be called in order of lottery numbers.

• Registrants who have held deferments in classes 1-D-D, 2-D, 3-A, 4-B, and 4-F and have acquired "extended liability." They would form the "age 26 selection group," the "age 27 selection group," and so on to the "age 34 selection group." If called, they would be drafted in order of lottery numbers.

• Registrants in the age 19 selection group, in order

of lottery numbers.

•Registrants in the age 18 selection group (ages 18½ to 19), in order of dates of birth, oldest first.

In the past, Selective Service hasn't reached beyond age 26 for draftees—at least not since World War II.

The "callup" procedures can be very confusing. If you have trouble understanding them, talk to your draft counselor.

Induction Orders

With a lottery number of 27 and a cutoff number of 100, your chances of being called for induction would be nearly 100%. This would be true even if you qualify for a deferment or exemption, like CO status. The reason is that all classification would take place *after* you'd been called for induction.

Your induction notice would tell you that you'd been placed in Class 1-A. It would give you at least ten days from its mailing date to report for induction. It would tell you where to report and what to do if for some reason you couldn't report or wanted to transfer your place of induction so you wouldn't have to travel hundreds of miles for induction. It would explain the induction procedures. And it would tell you how to apply for a new classification.

Applying for a New Classification

Your induction order will not contain any form for applying for a dferment or exemption. Instead, it will tell you to go to the Post Office and pick up a copy of Selective Service's "Classification Information Booklet." With the booklet, you will find a copy of SSS Form 9 (Request for Postponement, Deferment, or Exemption). This form does not require complete claims; you only have to fill in the correct boxes on the form to make your initial claim.

Your claim would have to be submitted *before* the date you are scheduled to report for induction. This would be your first chance to apply for any classification other than 1-A. Because you'd only be entitled to a minimum of ten days' notice of your reporting date, you'd have to act quickly. Your ten days' notice would begin on the *issue date* of your induction order. To meet the deadline, you'd have to *postmark* your claim before your reporting date. This would make your claim "timely" under the law. Though they should accept such a claim, Selective Service employees in the past have sometimes mistakenly refused to process claims and appeals which were timely but reached them after a deadline.

If the Post Office doesn't have the Classification Information Booklet, you can apply for deferment using a brief letter. If you are planning to apply for CO status, the minimum letter you should submit would read as follows: "I am by reason of my training and belief a conscientious objector to participation in war in any form. Please send me any necessary forms." This claim presents what in law is called a *prima facie* case—a claim that, on its face, would make you a CO if it were true.

The draft regulations say that you must submit all your deferment and exemption claims at the same time. If you submit one claim, you can't submit a second claim (for instance, for a hardship deferment) at a later time unless there is a change in your situation between the time you submit your first claim and the time you submit your second (for example, the death of someone in your family might be grounds for a hardship claim that you didn't make at first). If you're on a long postponement of induction—e.g., to allow you to finish your school term—it's not clear whether you can submit new claims once you've made your first group of claims. It's best to see a draft counselor if you're in this situation.

You can see that it's a good idea to have your claim(s) ready in advance. This is especially true with a CO application, but applications for classifications like 3-A (hardship or dependency deferment) and even 4-A (veteran) need a great deal of documentation in some cases.

If you're applying for conscientious objector status, your local board should automatically schedule you for a personal appearance to discuss your claim. But if you're applying for some other "judgmental" classification, like 3-A, you should ask for a personal appearance at the time you make your claim.

Classification Procedures

Once you've made a claim for deferment or exemption, Selective Service must postpone your induction date while they consider your requests. If your induction date is near, and you haven't received a postponement, get in touch with your draft counselor, your lawyer, or CCCO for advice on what you should do.

Your physical examination is supposed to take place on the date of your induction. If you claim a deferment, however, you may be ordered for a physical examination before your local board acts on your classification. If so, you should be careful that you aren't processed for induction by mistake. You can't always count on draft or military officials to be fair or to know what they're doing. It's best to take a copy of your postponement of induction with you and

You and the Draft—27

to get in touch with your draft counselor or attorney *immediately* if there's any misunderstanding. You can't actually be inducted unless you take part in the induction ceremony.

The first step in classification is for you to be assigned to a local board. Selective Service will place you under a local board which has jurisdiction over the last permanent address which you gave them. You can ask for a change of local board at the time you request a personal appearance. There's no guarantee, however, that your request will be granted. If you want to request a change of local board, it's best to give strong reasons for your request—for instance, that you're away for a year at school. If you don't ask for a different local board, or if your request is denied, your original local board will be your permanent local board.

Your local board must decide which classification you fit into, and, if you fit into more than one, they must place you in the "lowest" classification you're eligible for. If you've applied for an "administrative" classification, a Selective Service Area Office will make the first decision on your claim. However, if the Area Office denies your claim, you can appeal to your local board.

The classifications are arranged in a "hierarchy," as follows:

- 1-A-0—Conscientious objector to combatant military duty, available for induction as a noncombatant only.
- 1-C—Military member on active duty or member of the National Oceanic and Atmospheric Administration or Public Health Service.
- 1-D-D—Deferment for certain military Reservists or members of ROTC units.

- **1-D-E** — Exemption for certain military Reservists or members of ROTC units.
- **1-H** — "Holding" category for registrants who have not yet been called for induction.
- **1-O** — Conscientious objector to combatant and noncombatant military duty, available for civilian alternative service.
- **1-W** — Conscientious objector performing alternative service.
- **2-D** — Student preparing for the ministry.
- **3-A** — Registrant deferred because of hardship to dependents.
- **4-A** — Registrant who has completed military duty.
- **4-B** — Government official deferred by law.
- **4-C** — Alien or dual national not subject to induction.
- **4-D** — Minister of religion.
- **4-F** — Registrant not qualified for military duty on physical, mental, or moral grounds.
- **4-G** — Surviving son in a family where the father or one or more sisters or brothers were killed in action or died as the result of service-connected injuries after December 31, 1959; OR *only* surviving son in a family where the father or one or more sisters or brothers were killed in action or died as the result of military-connected injuries at any time. Does not apply in time of war or national emergency declared by Congress.
- **4-T** — Alien not subject to induction because his country has a treaty with the U.S. exempting each others' nationals from the draft in the other country.
- **4-W** — Conscientious objector who has completed alternative service.

Classes 1-A-O, 1-O, 2-D, 3-A, and 4-D are "judgmental" classifications which must be decided by your local board.

All of these classifications will be decided on the

basis of documentation that you submit. If denied, you have the right to appeal, and Selective Service must give reason(s) for their action. CCCO can give you more information on these classifications and what documents you'll need to establish your case.

Your Rights

If you apply for a deferment or exemption, you have several important rights to due process of law. For your own protection, it's important for you to know these rights and to exercise them.

- You have the right to a personal appearance before your local board.
- You have the right to present at least three witnesses to your local board to support your claim.
- You have the right to be accompanied to your personal appearance by an "advisor." Your advisor is not a witness. He or she can be an attorney or draft counselor. Your advisor can't address the board, but can confer with you to help you deal with confusing questions or other problems. Your local board can ask your advisor to leave the room if it feels he or she is "disrupting" the "informal" nature of the personal appearance.
- If your claim is denied, your local board must give its reasons for the denial in writing.
- If your claim is denied, you have the right to appeal to the District Appeal Board.
- You have the right to a personal appearance before the District Appeal Board.
- If the District Appeal Board denies your claim, they must give their reason(s) for the denial in writing.
- If one or more members of the District Appeal Board does not agree with the denial of your claim,

you have the right to appeal to the National Selective Service Appeal Board ("The President").

- You have the right to a personal appearance before the National Selective Service Appeal Board.
- If the National Appeal Board denies your claim, they must give their reason(s) for the denial in writing.
- You have the right to examine your file at your local board office.

Your Personal Appearance

If you're applying for conscientious objector status, your local board will automatically schedule you for a personal appearance. If you don't go to your personal appearance, you will be given another chance to appear. If you again don't appear, the local board will "deem" your claim to be withdrawn. Your local board can excuse a failure to appear if you provide a good reason—e.g., that you were ill—within five days after you failed to appear. It's best, of course, to appear. But if you can't make it to your personal appearance, you should send the local board a full explanation, certified mail, return receipt requested, and ask for a new appearance date.

Your local board will probably decide on your claim only once, based on your claim, your supporting letters, and your personal appearance. If they deny your claim, you won't have any further chance to appear before them—though you'll still have the right to appeal and to appear before the District Appeal Board.

Your personal appearance is your chance to present your claim and show that you're sincere. You'll probably be asked some difficult questions. It's not important to have answers to those questions. In fact, it's often better not to. If, for instance, you haven't worked out a complete stand on the use of force, that doesn't matter. Answer as best you can, and, if you find a question hard, say so. The important thing is to make clear that you object to war. Often a sincere statement that you haven't worked out all your ideas gives a better impression than a glib answer.

It's probably best to dress neatly and present as good an appearance as you can. Some COs get haircuts before their personal appearances; others don't. There's no way to tell which is the best idea. You should dress and appear as you feel most comfortable.

You might want to get some of your friends to fire questions at you, much the way your local board will do. This will give you practice in expressing your beliefs and, if your friends are good actors, dealing with your local board's hostility.

When you appear before your local board, you have the right to present three witnesses. The best witness is the kind of person who is also best to write a supporting letter. For more on supporting letters and who qualifies to write them, see Chapter 7.

It's a good idea to take an advisor with you to your personal appearance, as is your right. Your advisor can be your attorney or your draft counselor. He or she should be someone who knows the draft law and is familiar with your claim. If your local board asks you a tricky question, you have the right to confer with your advisor. Your advisor, however, can't speak for you.

If you don't speak English well, you should ask for an interpreter. You are allowed to have one. And, though an attorney can't speak for you before your local board, you can have an attorney appear as a witness.

Recording devices and verbatim transcripts (like

that made by a court reporter) are not permitted at personal appearances. You can, however, write down from memory a summary of what was said at your personal appearance. And you should. Your local board will file its own summary, and you should give your point of view on what happened. The summary should be in dialogue form if you can remember that well. Your witnesses can help you to remember and corroborate your account. When you've completed your summary, make a copy of it for your own records, get it notarized if you can, and send it to your local board for your file. You should also look at your draft file to see what your local board says about your personal appearance.

The Appeal Process

Once you've submitted your claim to your local board, they will act on it—probably the day or night you appear. If they deny your claim, you should receive a notice of denial, along with a statement of their reason(s). You will have fifteen days from the mailing date of your denial to appeal to the District Appeal Board.

Along with your appeal, if you want it, you should send a request for a personal appearance before the Appeal Board. Remember to send all letters, appeals, etc., by certified mail, return receipt requested. The postmark on your letter determines whether you have met the necessary deadline.

At the personal appearance before the District Appeal Board, you have some of the same rights as you did when appearing before your local board. You can present evidence to support your claim. And you can have an advisor with you. You have no right to witnesses, however.

Following your appearance before the District Appeal Board, you will again receive a notice of their decision on your claim. If your claim is denied, the Appeal Board must give its reason(s). If the decision of the Appeal Board is unanimous, you have no further appeal, and you can expect to receive a notice of your new induction date.

If one or more members of the Appeal Board disagree with the denial of your claim, you have the right to appeal to "The President,' within fifteen days of the mailing of your notice of denial. Appeals to the President are handled by the National Selective Service Appeal Board. Again, you have the right to request a personal appearance before this board.

When you appear before the National Appeal Board, you again have the right to present evidence to support your claim. And you can have an advisor, just as you did before the local and appeal boards. You again have no right to present witnesses.

Following denial by the National Appeal Board, or unanimous denial by the District Appeal Board, there is no formal appeal. If you find yourself at the end of your formal appeals, consult your draft counselor right away. There may be further steps you can take.

Replying to Reasons

When your local board gives its reason(s) for denying your claim, they also give you a chance to strengthen your claim where it's weak. A good reply to the local board's reason(s) for denying your claim may convince the Appeal Board to grant the claim, or it may help if your case ends in court.

Because the "reasons" requirement wasn't followed by all local boards until 1971, draft counselors don't have much experience to guide them in talking about replying to local board reasons. No one knows, for instance, whether local board reasons in the future are likely to be very general or very specific.

But a few suggestions may be helpful. If your local board's reason for denying your claim is very general (for instance, in a CO claim, "we find the registrant insincere"),* you can only reply to it by strengthening your whole claim (for instance, by providing more supporting letters and having your witnesses write further letters of support) and pointing out how vague the reason is. If your local board points out a real weakness in your claim, you should deal specifically with that weakness. For example, if you've been in Junior ROTC and haven't explained before how your views have changed since then, your reply to the local board is a good time to deal with this point.

You and your draft counselor should discuss the local board's reason(s) for denying your claim. Your reply should be sent certified mail, return receipt requested. If you find the reasons hard to reply to because they're too general, say so. You don't have to be defensive in your reply, and this is one way of taking the offensive.

Even though you may have no further appeal from the Appeal Board's decision, write a reply anyway and submit it to your file. It could help if your case ends up in court.

Your reply to the local board (and your reply to the Appeal Board) can also contain new information which

---

*This reason is actually an illegal reason because it is too vague. The courts have made this clear in recent rulings on COs who were trying to obtain discharge from the military. But you should try to reply to even a vague reason like this one by strengthening your claim.

you think will help your claim. You can point out local or Appeal Board errors—for instance, not giving you enough time to present your case. And you can mention local board hostility or anger if you think it was unreasonable.

Induction

If your claim has been denied at all levels, or if you don't request a reclassification, you will be required to report for induction. Following your appeals, your postponement of induction will expire, and you will receive notice of a new reporting date. If you don't report, you will be given another chance to show up, and if you still don't report, you'll be turned over to the Justice Department for possible prosecution.

Induction processing includes a complete Armed Forces mental test, a check of your criminal record (if you have one), and a complete Armed Forces physical examination. If you fail the physical, you will be classified 4-F but you could be re-examined in the future (it's not likely, though). If the military can't determine whether you're qualified for military duty, you could be sent home and called back for re-examination and possible induction in a month or so. If you have a medical condition which should cause you to fail the physical, it's important for you to have proof with you when you go for induction. The military seldom finds conditions if you don't point them out.

If you pass the military examinations, you'll face the choice of accepting or refusing induction. In most cases, you'll have to do one or the other before you can get your case to court. For details, see Chapter 14.

If you've decided to refuse induction, you do so during the induction ceremony. To avoid confusion, it's best to tell the induction center officials in advance that you're going to refuse.

During the induction ceremony, all the draftees being inducted that day line up and are told to step forward. If you step forward, you become a member of the military. If you don't step forward, you have refused induction. You'll probably be taken aside and given another chance to step forward, warned of the legal consequences of what you're doing, etc. You might be arrested, but this is rare. In most cases, once you've made clear that you aren't going to change your mind, you'll be sent home to wait for prosecution.

Do not confuse the induction ceremony with the oath of allegiance. The oath takes place only *after* you are a member of the military. If you step forward but refuse to take the oath, you will remain a member of the military and you will have to seek a discharge or use a writ of habeas corpus to challenge your induction order in court.

If you plan to refuse induction, CCCO recommends that you go to the induction center rather than simply failing to report. It's just possible that you'll fail the physical examination, or that military officials will make an error in your processing that could lead to an acquittal in court. And by going to the induction center, you make sure that you've "exhausted your administrative remedies." The courts require you to do this before they'll hear your case. ("Exhausting your administrative remedies" also includes appealing the denial of your claim.)

If Your Claim Is Accepted

If you make a CO claim and it is accepted, you'll be subject to one of two kinds of duty: noncombatant military duty if you're a 1-A-0, or alternative civilian duty if you're 1-0. Noncombatant COs are ordered for induction just like other draftees. To avoid confusion, it's important that you have proof of your noncombatant status when you report for induction. For details on what noncombatants do, see Part V.

If you're granted 1-0 status, you'll be required to perform civilian work "in lieu of induction." For more on alternative service, see Chapter 8.

PART II

WAR RESISTANCE AND THE LAW

CHAPTER 4
REGISTRATION AND RESISTANCE

If you're a man eighteen or nearing that age, you'll have to decide whether or not to register for the draft. Women aren't included under the current draft law, but Congress could change that at any time. Man or woman, it's best for you to think now about registration and draft resistance. This chapter explains what's involved, why some people have resisted, and some other ways people have resisted war. It also gives guidelines that may help you think through your own stand.

The Law on Registration

The Military Selective Service Act requires male U.S. citizens aged 18 through 26 to register for the draft when the President orders them to do so. Many foreign citizens who live in the U.S. are also required to register.*

The President can proclaim registration days by Executive Order if he thinks that a draft registration is

---

*The law on registration of aliens is very complex. If you're a foreign citizen, consult a draft counselor or attorney who knows the draft law for the latest information.

needed. Or he can set up a "continuing" registration. An example of the first was the two-week registration held in July, 1980, for men born in 1960 and 1961. An example of the second was the registration requirement in effect from 1948 to 1974, when all men were required to register at the time they reached 18.

At present, all men are required to register for the draft within a sixty-day period that begins thirty days before their 18th birthdays—that is, within thirty days before or twenty-nine days after their 18th birthdays.

A draft registration can be held whether or not inductions are taking place. For instance, no inductions are taking place now, but men are still required to register.

WARNING: The details on registration, who must register, when they must register, etc., can change quickly. Do not rely on this chapter alone. Consult CCCO or your draft counselor for the latest information.

Registration Procedures

If you're included among those who must register, you'll be required to go to the Post Office and fill in a Registration Form (SSS Form 3). A copy of this form will be found on p. 43.

Once you've filled in the Registration Form, a postal clerk will check to see that it's legible and then forward it to Selective Service. Your name will then be placed on Selective Service's computer listing of registrants for your year of birth.

WARNING: The Postal Service often loses mail. To protect yourself, make a copy of your completed Registration Form. Keep copies of everything you send to Selective Service.

Sometime after you register, Selective Service will

SELECTIVE SERVICE SYSTEM
Registration Form
READ PRIVACY ACT STATEMENT ON REVERSE
PLEASE PRINT CLEARLY

—DO NOT WRITE IN THE ABOVE SPACE—

1 DATE OF BIRTH
Name of Month | Day | Year

2 SEX
☐ MALE
☐ FEMALE

3 SOCIAL SECURITY NUMBER
___ ___ ___ — ___ ___ — ___ ___ ___ ___

4 PRINT FULL NAME
Last | First | Middle

5 CURRENT MAILING ADDRESS
Number and Street
City | State or Foreign Country | Zip Code

6 PERMANENT RESIDENCE (If different than BLOCK 5)
Number and Street
City | State or Foreign Country | Zip Code

7 CURRENT TELEPHONE NUMBER
Area Code | Number

8 I AFFIRM THE FOREGOING STATEMENTS ARE TRUE
Today's Date | Signature of Registrant
(Previous Editions Will Not Be Used And Will Be Destroyed)

Postal Date Stamp & Clerk Initials
☐ ID
☐ NO ID
☐ OTHER

SSS FORM 1 (JAN 82)

OMB Approval 3240-0002

send you a Registration Acknowledgement (SSS Form 3A). This form lets them check to see that they have correct information on you. If their information is correct, you don't have to return the form. You may want to do so, however, following the procedure suggested under "Your Choices," below.

Filling Out the Registration Form

The Registration Form asks for your name, address, date of birth, and Social Security Number. If you're unsure on any point, or if you still haven't decided whether you want to register, you have a legal right to take the form home and study it or discuss it with your draft counselor.

If you register, the Selective Service System can send your name to a military recruiter whether you want them to or not. You can't stop them from doing this, but you can write a note on the Registration Form saying that you object to having your name sent to a recruiter.

WARNING: Postal clerks often tell registrants that they have no right to take the Registration Form home. This is not true. If you run into any problem, call CCCO or your draft counselor for help.

The instructions on the Registration Form and the Registration Acknowledgement say that you must fill in all the information requested, including your Social Security Number. If you object to giving Selective Service your Social Security Number, call CCCO or your draft counselor *before* you register to get information and ideas on how to protect yourself. The courts have ruled that Selective Service can require you to give your Social Security Number.

Selective Service does not now issue registration or classification cards, so your own record of the

Registration Form and the Registration Acknowledgement may be the only proof you'll have that you registered. You can, however, ask the Director of Selective Service for evidence of your registration once every six months.

Your Choices

If you are required to register for the draft, you have six choices:

• *You can refuse to register and tell Selective Service, the President, the newspapers, etc., thus taking a public stand.* This action violates the draft law. It increases your chances of facing prosecution. But you may want to do it to make a point about registration and the draft. In the past, thousands of people have publicly refused to register with just this idea in mind.

• *You can refuse to register and tell no one.* This "private" resistance also violates the law. But you're not as likely to be prosecuted as you would be if you took a public stand. If you object to registering but don't feel you want to make a public witness about it, this position may be the right one for you. Or you may simply feel that the government has no right to arrest you, and you don't have to help them. Either way, you shouldn't decide not to register because you don't think you'll be caught. Always think first about the worst that could happen, and whether you could face it, before you break the law. If you resist in this way, you may want to write a statement of your reasons and place it in your personal file (see Chapter 7) in case you are prosecuted in the future.

• *You can register for the draft under protest.* Many peace groups have stickers which you can attach to your registration form, or you can just write your protest in the margin of the Registration Form. This position is legal. Selective Service will ignore your protest, but you will at least be on record against the draft. Stickers can be peeled off, so you're safest writing your protest in the margin of the card.

•*You can register as a conscientious objector.* Again, some peace groups have stickers which you can attach to your registration form, or you can just write your claim in the margin and make a copy of your card for your records. It is legal to register as a conscientious objector. A simple statement like, "I am a conscientious objector to war in any form" is best. Selective Service will *not* process your claim or even acknowledge it. But you'll at least be on record. Again, keep in mind that stickers can be peeled off the Registration Form.

•*You can simply register, leaving your CO application—or your decision on whether you want to file an application—for later.* You can't hurt a later CO claim by doing this. As you've seen in Chapter 3, Selective Service rules don't even allow you to file for conscientious objector status until you're called for induction. Draft officials can't deny your claim because you followed the rules they themselves set up. It's important, however, for you to make your decision and begin gathering supporting evidence as soon as you can.

•*You can register and make a CO statement with your Registration Acknowledgement.* When you receive your Registration Acknowledgement, you can return it, certified mail, return receipt requested, with a brief statement of your objection to war. Selective Service won't process this claim. Instead, they'll probably return it to you. But you'll still have a record that you tried to file. This could help a later claim.

Resisting After Registration

If you decide to resist after you've registered, there isn't much you can do to get your name off Selective Service's computer list. Resisters in the past have returned their draft cards, refused to fill out forms that Selective Service sent them, etc. You could refuse to return the Registration Acknowledgement, but if you do, Selective Service will merely assume that your address is correct. If you decide to resist after you've registered, you may not be able to do so until inductions begin again. But you can go on record against the draft by sending back your Registration Verification with a statement of protest. And if you're called for induction, you can refuse induction.

No registration cards will be issued under current procedures. So, if you want to resist, you can't send your cards back to Selective Service. You won't have any to sent back.

Why Resist?

This *Handbook* can't tell you whether you should be a conscientious objector or resist the draft. You'll have to live with your decision, so you must, and should, decide for yourself what to do. But in the past, people have resisted the draft for many reasons.

Nearly all draft resisters object to war. Their views on war aren't that much different from the views of people who apply for legal conscientious objector status—if they're different at all. But resisters often see the draft as part of the war system and believe it's important for them to refuse any kind of support for war that they can. This idea has strong arguments to support it. As you've seen in Chapter 2, the draft supplies manpower for the military when it is inducting people, and it helps to keep the military ready for combat even there are no inductions. Some draft resisters object to conscription itself. They believe the government shouldn't have the right to draft people. In England during the Second World War there were even resisters who supported the war but felt it should be fought with volunteers. You can object to conscription and war all at once, of course, and most resisters do.

One reason for objecting to the draft is because it discriminates against the poor, minorities, and those with less education. This is certainly true. If you read over the chapters on applying for conscientious objector status, you'lll see that the draft rules favor people who read and write well. Even if you don't read and write well you can apply for and get CO status. But many people simply give up. Or they don't know they can apply. Minority people have less chance than others in our society to get a good education or a good job. And when there's a war, the people who have had fewer civilian opportunities often end up in the front lines.

Some resisters think that, by taking conscientious objector status, they would simply be helping the system to operate. They would be opening up a place for someone else to be drafted. Again, this is true enough. Unless the U.S. disbands its military or cuts back on defense, the military will get the people it needs, come what may. If there's a draft, it will get them by drafting them. And if there are a lot of COs, draft quotas will probably increase.

Finally, some resisters don't qualify for conscientious objector status at all. This is true, for instance, of people who object to only one war, such as Vietnam. If you don't object to all wars, you may decide to resist the draft. Or you could follow the suggestions in

Chapter 6 and make your CO claim anyway. Either way, you may find that your conscience leads you to break the law—either by refusing to register or by refusing induction. But don't assume that you don't qualify for CO status until you've read the rest of this *Handbook*.

None of this means that you should resist. There are good reasons for resisting the draft, but there are also good reasons for not resisting it. What you do will depend on your values, your situation, your feelings about what you're ready to face, and many other factors.

Penalties

Refusing to register for the draft is a violation of the draft law. It is a felony. If the government prosecutes you, you could be punished with up to five years in federal prison or up to $10,000 fine or both. This may also be true of refusing to report a change of address or other "minor" violations. But the government isn't likely to go after you for "minor" draft violations.

Not all resisters face prosecution. Of those who do, few receive the maximum penalty. But prison is always a possibility if you resist the draft.

For more information on court procedures and prison, see Part IV of this *Handbook*.

Resisting War in Other Ways

Even if you don't refuse to register, you may want to know about ways to resist war. Refusing induction, as described in Chapter 3, is a way of resisting the draft and war. Here are two others that draft resisters often use.

Civil Disobedience

Many war resisters believe that laws which make war possible are immoral. They're willing to break the law to help bring about peace. Often on demonstrations, for instance, some of the demonstrators will cross police lines that they believe are wrong. During the 1950s, war resisters sometimes entered nuclear test sites and were arrested.

Most people who break the law in this way expect to be arrested. They take their stand as a way of showing the public that the laws they are breaking are wrong or wrongly applied. Civil disobedience has been used by labor unions, the independence movement in India, the civil rights movement of the 1960s, and the anti-nuclear-power movement in addition to the peace movement. For more information, check some of the books under "Further Reading" at the end of this *Handbook*.

War Tax Resistance

One way to resist war is to refuse to pay for it. War tax resisters believe that it's wrong for them to pay taxes when over half of the federal budget goes for the military. They usually don't face jail because the Internal Revenue Service can get the taxes they owe, plus interest and penalties, by attaching their bank accounts or property.

War tax resistance and the tax laws are very complex. You shouldn't refuse to pay your taxes without talking to a good tax resistance counselor. CCCO can help you to find one if you decide you object to war taxes.

Thinking About Resistance

No one but you can decide whether you should resist the draft. Here are some guidelines to help you think about your position:

• *Think about yourself.* What do you need to do to live with your conscience? If you resist, do you think you could face jail? What are your most important values?

• *Think about others.* There's nothing wrong or unusual about being concerned with your family. How would your resistance affect them? If you're married, how would it affect your marriage? Your children? Do you think it's worth the risk? Many do; others don't. Neither position is "wrong."

• *There is no one right position.* Many people have resisted the draft; many others have not. Often their views on war were pretty much the same. Resisters aren't "better" than people who decide to apply for CO status. And you won't be "worse," whichever road you take.

• *No one can be perfect.* Living in modern society is a compromise. If you resist the draft, you may still find that resisting taxes is not for you. And even if you resist the draft and the income tax, you may still pay federal taxes on gasoline—which support a highway system designed partly to help troop movements. You can't really avoid contributing to the military in some way. What you can do is decide in which ways you definitely *won't* contribute.

• *Talk about your position.* It's a good idea to talk with several people as you decide what to do. Talk with people who support resistance, with people who are against it, with your family, and with your draft counselor. You have to make your own choice, but other people can sometimes help you to see things more clearly.

- *Don't be afraid to follow the law.* There's nothing "wrong" about following the law, and you don't need to feel guilty if that's your decision. Many people who object to war do register for the draft and apply for conscientious objector status. Sometimes people who support resistance will tell you this is a "cop-out," but it isn't. It's another way of expressing beliefs about war which are much the same as those of resisters. And there may be good reasons—like your family situation—why you shouldn't resist.
- *Don't be afraid to resist.* If you decide to break the law, you'll have plenty of support. You can get help from the peace movement, from your friends, from your family, and from CCCO. If you're a member of a church, your church or minister will probably respect your conscience and help you. Even if you end in prison, you can get visits from your family and from Prisoner Visitation and Support Committee (see Chapter 15).

The choice on whether to resist the draft is yours. Before you make it, you should read the rest of this *Handbook*. You'll find it helpful to know just what's involved in legal conscientious objection, and some of the later chapters will help you to think about war, court, and prison. To resist or not to resist is a decision you shouldn't make without a lot of thought. The remaining chapters in this *Handbook*, and the books under "Further Reading," can give you a start.

CHAPTER 5
CONSCIENTIOUS OBJECTION UNDER THE LAW

If you're against war and believe it would be wrong for you to be part of it, you may qualify as a conscientious objector under the draft law. Section 6(j) of the Military Selective Service Act provides exemption for conscientious objectors to war. It reads in part:

> Nothing contained in this [Act] shall ... require any person to be subject to combatant training and service in the Armed Forces of the United States who, by reason of religious training and belief, is conscientiously opposed to participation in war in any form. As used in this subsection, the term "religious training and belief" does not include essentially political, sociological, or philosophical views, or a merely personal moral code. Any person claiming exemption from combatant training and service because of such conscientious objection whose claim is sustained by the local board shall, if he is inducted into the Armed Forces under this [Act], be assigned to noncombatant service ... or shall, if he is found to be conscientiously opposed to such noncombatant service, in lieu of induction, be ordered by his local board, subject to such regulations as the President may prescribe, to

perform for a period [of two years] ... civilian work contributing to the maintenance of the national health, safety, or interest.

But What Does It Mean?

Section 6(j) is hard even for attorneys and judges to understand. But the basic standards for conscientious objectors are simple. The Supreme Court summarized them in *Clay v. U.S.* (1971). A conscientious objector under the law, the Court said, must:
- Be "religious," as the Supreme Court has defined this word (see below);
- Object to all wars; and
- Be sincere in his or her application.

Your job, if you decide to apply for CO status, will be to convince your local board that you meet these standards. If you've made a good application, your local board then can't turn you down unless they have good reasons for doing so. For more information on making a good claim, see Chapter 7.

"Religion" and the Law

To qualify as a conscientious objector, you must base your claim on "religious training and belief." But this *doesn't* mean you have to be religious *as most of us use that word.* In *U.S. v. Seeger* (1965), the Supreme Court said that a religious belief is "a sincere and meaningful" belief that "occupies a place in the life of its possessor parallel to that filled by [an] orthodox belief in God." You can base your CO claim on a traditional religion, like Christianity, or on some other belief that has the same place in your life. As long as your claim is based on a belief that is central to you, you can qualify as a conscientious objector. Your belief can be religious, moral, or ethical—or a mixture belief can be religious, moral, or ethical—or a mixture of all three. You don't have to believe in God or attend church. And in a later case, *Welsh v. U.S.* (1970), the Supreme Court said that you don't even have to call your belief religious.

Whether or not you think of yourself as religious, filing for CO status, or thinking about conscientious objection, means thinking about your most important beliefs and feelings. Do you believe in a god? What do you believe about your god? Or about your own place in the world and the universe? Questions like these are important as you decide whether to file for CO status and as you prepare yourself to file.

Even though the law doesn't require a traditional religious claim, it's useful to know what some thinkers have said about religion and its relation to moral choices. Paul Tillich, the well-known Lutheran theologian, spoke of:

> [T]he "God above God," the power of being, which works through those who have no name for it, not even the name God.

John Woolman, a Quaker anti-slavery activist, said:

> There is a principle which is pure, placed in the human mind, which in different places and ages hath had different names. ... It is deep and inward, confined to no forms of religion, nor excluded from any. ... In whomsoever this takes root and grows, of what nation soever, they become brethren.

Religion, say these writers, does not have to be called "religious." Martin Luther King, Jr., added:

> It really boils down to this: that all life is

interrelated. ... Whatever affects one directly, affects all indirectly. We are made to live together because of the interrelated structure of reality.

And David Saville Muzzey, a well-known Ethical Culture thinker, said, "Religion ... must surely mean the devotion of man to the highest idea that he can conceive."

What is *your* highest ideal? How does it lead you to oppose war? These are questions you need to ask yourself as you think about conscientious objection.

If you're a member of a church, even one of the traditional "peace churches," you still need to think hard about what you believe. Under the law, it's your individual belief, not the beliefs of your church, that counts. When you apply for CO status, it's not enough to say, for instance, that you are a Quaker. And it's not enough to quote your church's creed. How does your creed lead you to be a CO? Even in the "peace churches," many church members join the military. Why not you? You need to know, and, if you apply for CO status, your local board will want to know.

Religious Training

Many COs worry that they won't be able to show any religious training when they apply for CO status. Even if you've never been to church or Sunday School, however, this is less of a problem than you may think. How did you come to your belief? The answer to this question, under the law, *is* your religious training. Your training is the background to the beliefs you have.

This means that you don't have to show you went to Sunday School unless it affected the way you believe now. You don't have to show anything other than how you came to the belief you have. It's important to think clearly about how you became a CO—both for your local board and for yourself. For ideas on how to show *your* training, see Chapter 7.

War in Any Form

To qualify as a conscientious objector, you must object to "war in any form." This doesn't mean that you have to oppose all use of force. You have to object to "real shooting wars," wars as common sense used the word. Any other beliefs you have are important, but they don't have any bearing on your CO claim.

Some COs don't know what they would do in the future—or what they would have done in the past. If you're in this situation, you may still qualify as a CO who objects to "war in any form." During the Vietnam era, many COs applied to their draft boards using an "existential" approach. What, they asked themselves, do I believe here and now? Do I really know that my beliefs will be different in the future? Or can I leave that for the future? These are good questions to ask yourself.

The next chapter explains in more detail what is meant by "war in any form." And if you don't know where you stand on this question, you may find Part III helpful also.

"Deeply Held" Beliefs

COs and local boards are often confused because Selective Service directives say that a CO's beliefs must be both sincere *and* "deeply held." What does "deeply held" mean? How do you show that your beliefs are "deeply held"? Are some beliefs "deeper" than others?

It's hard to understand, but, luckily, you don't have to. The courts have held that your local board can't deny your claim because your beliefs are not "deeply held" enough. " 'Depth of conviction,' " said one court, "requires theological or philosophical speculation. We think it unwise to adopt this more complex concept as the requirement which a Selective Service registrant ... must fulfill in order to qualify for conscientious objector classification."

For purposes of law, sincerity is enough. Are you what you claim to be? That's the only question you need to answer. Your local board can't say that you are what you claim to be, but don't feel strongly enough about it.

Personal Moral Code

Section 6(j) seems to say that you can't be a CO if you oppose war because of a "merely personal moral code." If you have trouble understanding how this is different from a moral objection to war, you're not alone. In philosophy and in the law as interpreted by the courts, there's no real difference between a personal moral code and a moral belief about war.

All moral beliefs are personal. If you believe that you should not be part of war, that's a personal decision, even if you base your decision on your church's teachings. Few churches require their members to be COs. And whether you're a church member or not, war is a matter between you and your conscience. Your CO beliefs are your personal beliefs. But they also qualify as "religious" beliefs if they are central to your life. Keep this in mind, and you won't get confused if your local board says you have a "merely personal moral code."

Political Beliefs

Like most COs or people who are against war, you probably have ideas about politics, U.S. foreign policy, the defense budget, the draft, and many other issues. You may consider your beliefs political—not religious or moral.

But if you object to all war, there's a good chance that you have a belief which qualifies as "religious" under the law. Your local board can't deny your CO claim unless the *sole* basis for it is political. Before you disqualify yourself, think about why you hold the political beliefs that you do.

Suppose, for instance, that you object to war because it's a way for the rich to oppress the poor. This seems to be a political objection, but it may not be. Why do you think it's wrong for the rich to oppress the poor? What's wrong with injustice? The values that lead you to think that injustice is wrong may also qualify as the basis for a CO claim.

You may find that your beliefs have no religious, moral, or ethical basis at all. That's pretty unlikely, but if it's true, you're disqualified from CO status as the law now reads. But you can still file a CO claim. Your local board may think you *do* have a set of values which qualifies. And you'll at least be on record as to what you believe if you should decide to resist the draft.

Are You Sincere?

Many COs wonder not only how they can show their sincerity, but how their local boards can judge it.

If you present a CO claim that meets the legal standards, the burden of proving that you don't qualify falls on your local board. They can't deny your claim merely because they suspect you are lying. "[D]oubt as to sincerity cannot be [based] on mere speculation." They will be looking for behavior that is inconsistent with your claim—for example, fighting if you claim to be nonviolent. They will look at your own story of how you became a CO. They should read your supporting letters, though local boards often don't. And, when you appear before them, they will be looking at you. If they find evidence that shows you are not telling the truth, they will deny your claim.

You can go a long way toward convincing your local board by presenting a good CO claim. Chapter 7 will help you to do this.

"Late" Claims

Because you now can't file for CO status until you are called for induction, "late" filing (filing long after you've registered for the draft) shouldn't be as much of a problem as it used to be. You *can't* make a CO claim when you register, though you can follow the suggestions in the last chapter to get yourself on record. And it's a good idea to do so.

But even if you haven't put yourself on record before you file your formal CO claim, you local board can't deny your CO claim because it is "late." The regulations don't allow any choice. And even if you only decide at the last minute that you're a CO, your local board can't turn you down solely because you haven't been a CO all your life.

It's best, of course, to decide as soon as possible and start building a file as described in Chapter 7. But you must make your own decision in your own way. If it takes time for you to do so, that's all right.

Two Types of COs

The law divides conscientious objectors into two types:

- If you object to war but are willing to serve in the military without weapons, your local board should put you in class 1-A-0.
- If you object to war and also object to being in the military at all, your local board should put you in class 1-0.

Both 1-A-0s and 1-0s must object to all wars. Both must be "religious" and sincere. If you ask for class 1-0, your local board can't give you 1-A-0 as a "compromise" unless they believe you really don't object to being in the military. And if you ask for 1-A-0, they must put you in class 1-0 if they find that you really are against being in the military.

The two kinds of objectors are very similar. The difference between them lies in where each draws his or her line. Most 1-A-0s think it is not wrong for them to serve in the military as long as they personally do not kill. 1-0s disagree and think it is wrong to serve in the military at all.

Local boards are more likely to give 1-A-0 status than 1-0 status because they know that 1-A-0s become soldiers. But you shouldn't apply for 1-A-0 status just because it's easier to get. If you feel you object to *any part* of being in the military, you should apply for 1-0 status.

How do you feel about wearing a military uniform? Following military orders? Being part of the military "chain of command"? If you object to any of these things, you should apply for 1-0 status.

For more information on what 1-A-0 soldiers do, see Part V. 1-0 COs do civilian alternative service if they would have been called for induction. See Chapter 8 for more information. And if you don't know which status applies to you, read Part V and talk to a draft counselor.

Thinking About War

In order to decide whether you're a conscientious objector, you need to think about war and what you believe. This chapter has explained the law on conscientious objection, but knowing the law isn't enough. In fact, the law can sometimes confuse the issue more than it helps. Before you decide whether you fit under the law, you need to think about where you fit into the war system—if you do at all. Chapter 6 and Part III of this *Handbook* should help you to think about your own beliefs.

CHAPTER 6
SELECTIVE OBJECTION

In the late 1960s and early 1970s, many people objected to the Vietnam war. Some also objected to all wars. Some did not know what they thought about other wars because they were concerned with stopping the war that was going on. And some said that they would fight under other conditions, but not in Vietnam.

This last group, called "selective objectors," is not granted CO status under current law. An important 1971 Supreme Court decision, *Gillette v. U.S.*, 401 U.S. 437, said that Congress didn't have to include them under the law. The court also said that restricting CO status to people who oppose all wars is constitutional.

Despite the Court's decision, the issue of selective objection won't go away. It's also not as new as it looks. In Britain during World War II, for instance, the law allowed selective objection. Some local tribunals (the British equivalent of a draft board) granted CO status to Welshmen who objected to fighting for Britain, to Italians who didn't want to fight fellow countrymen, and even to people who were pro-German. And some in the U.S. churches were discussing selective objection long before the Vietnam War. (See also "The Just War Theory," below.)

One reason the problem won't go away is the nature of modern war itself. Unless there is a full-scale nuclear war, chances are that many future wars will be counter-insurgency wars like Vietnam or the Soviet invasion of Afghanistan. And counter-insurgency war usually involves killing civilians, burning villages, and destroying crops—just as it did in Vietnam. For more about counter-insurgency war, see Chapter 9.

The Gillette Case

The Supreme Court's ruling in *Gillette* seems simple enough. Guy Gillette said that he objected to the Vietnam war but would fight in a United Nations police force or to defend the U.S. against direct attack. The Court ruled that he didn't qualify for CO status and that the law which kept him from being a CO was constitutional.

But deciding whether or not you're a selective objector is more difficult than it seems. The Court in *Gillette* said there is a difference between selective objectors and

> persons who oppose participating in all wars, but cannot say with complete certainty that their present convictions and existing state of mind are unalterable. See, e.g., *U.S. v. Owen*, 415 F.2d 383, 390 (8th Cir. 1969). Unwillingness to deny the possibility of a change of mind, in some hypothetical future circumstances, may be no more than humble good sense, casting no doubt on the claimant's present sincerity of belief.

The *Owen* case, which the Court cited, is even stronger. Owen had been asked by a hearing officer whether he would change his mind if the country were attacked. The hearing officer reported that Owen said he would. Owen denied this. The 8th Circuit Court said that *even if the hearing officer told the truth,* Owen's answer couldn't keep him from getting CO status because it didn't relate to the present. In effect, the Court said, the question doesn't mean anything. What counts is whether you *now* oppose all wars.

Owen may have said his views would change. Gillette said that, as his views were *now*, he would fight. That's the difference. If you find that hard to understand, don't worry. It's not a very clear distinction. A good rule of thumb is that if you're confused about what you'd do in a future war, you qualify as a conscientious objector. Only if you are sure that you would fight are you disqualified.

What about past wars? The *Gillette* case doesn't say anything about them, but a case decided later does. In *U.S. v. Stewart,* the Second Circuit Court of Appeals said that if you're unsure what you would have done, you're simply showing "humble good sense," and you can qualify for CO status. Another case, *U.S. v. Willson,* says that you have to be sure what you would have done. But the *Willson* case was decided before the *Gillette* case. It's safe to say that you don't have to be sure what you would have done as long as you're sure you *now* object to all wars.

Gray Areas

The problem with all these cases is that they're trying to draw black-and-white lines where there are only gray areas. If you're of draft age, you weren't even born until long after World War II. In fact, you weren't born until after the end of the "police action" in Korea. And unless you're psychic you don't really know what a future war would be like—only what it *might* be like. This is true whether you oppose all wars or only some wars.

So when the law says you must object to all wars, the best you can say is whether you oppose all wars *as far as you know*. You can't, for example, say what your beliefs would be if you were a guerilla fighter in Afghanistan. You can only look at war from your point of view and decide on your own stand. And that's all you have to do.

This doesn't mean that you can't look at history and learn from it, or criticize the actions of nations that go to war. You can. You may want to. Chances are you don't just object to war, you want to help stop it. But for purposes of the law, you don't have to know everything you will do or would have done in the past.

The Just War Theory

Many people who would have been selective objectors in the past now find that, in practice, they object to all wars. An example might be the classic Christian idea of the "just war." Two hundred years ago, Christians might have chosen to be part of one war, and not part of another, on the basis of this theory. Some still find that they can. But many others think that a "just war" is no longer possible. So they end up opposing all war.

Beginning with St. Augustine (354-430 A.D.), the Just War Theory tried to set up standards for deciding which wars were right and which wrong. As many theologians now put it, the standards are seven:

•War must be the last resort and used only after all other means have failed.

•War must be declared to redress rights actually violated or for defense against unjust demands backed

by the threat of force.
- The war must be openly and legally declared by a legal government.
- There must be a reasonable chance of winning.
- The means used must be in proportion to the ends sought.
- Soldiers must distinguish between armies and civilians and not kill civilians on purpose.
- The winner must not require the utter humiliation of the loser.

The Vietnam War violated at least six of these standards. It wasn't a last resort. The rights of the U.S. hadn't been violated, and the U.S. hadn't been attacked. The war was undeclared. Far from there being a chance of victory, no one in the government even knew what "victory" meant. The means—like dropping millions of tons of bombs on North Vietnam—were out of proportion to whatever end the war sought (except the total destruction of Vietnam). U.S. soldiers, under orders, killed thousands of civilians in "search-and-destroy" missions and similar operations. Nobody will ever know, of course, whether the U.S. wanted to humiliate the Vietnamese.

Modern wars usually break one or more of the Just War standards. In the Civil War, Sherman's March to the Sea (see Chapter 9) destroyed property and killed many civilians. In World War I, over a million soldiers might die in a six-month battle over less than a thousand yards of ground. In World War II, both sides bombed civilians, and the Allies demanded unconditional surrender (utter humiliation). And in a nuclear war, who can say that there would be a reasonable chance of winning?

That's why some people now think that a "just war" is impossible. At least one court case, *U.S. v. Berg*, has held that you can get CO status if you believe this. Berg based his CO claim on the Just War Theory and said that, since a "just war" is now impossible, he opposed all wars. The Court agreed.

Do you think a "just war" is possible now? That's a good question even if you don't follow the Just War Theory. If you don't believe there can be a just war, you may qualify for conscientious objector status.

If You Think You're Selective

As you've seen in this chapter and Chapter 5, the dividing line between a legally recognized CO and a "selective objector" isn't really as clear as it sounds. But what should you do if you think you are a selective objector? Here are some guidelines which may help.

•Decide whether you really are a selective objector. This means looking at the law, as this chapter has done, and thinking about your own beliefs. Don't exclude yourself too quickly. Part III of this *Handbook* may help you to be more clear about the moral issues. It's designed to start you thinking, wherever you come out.

•If you're a selective objector, think about what you object to and what you don't. Do you, for instance, support all wars except Vietnam? How do you decide?

•Even though you may not qualify under the law, apply for CO status anyway, unless you object to the draft and plan to resist it. There are a lot of reasons for doing this. Your draft board may conclude that you do qualify as a CO. The law may change. You'll be on record with a statement of your beliefs if you end up in court. And every application from a selective objector makes it more likely that selective objectors will be recognized in the future.

Support for Selective Objectors

Many church and civil liberties groups support the right to object to particular wars. In addition to CCCO, here's a partial list:

American Civil Liberties Union
National Council of Churches
Presbyterian Church in the U.S.
United Church of Christ
American Lutheran Church
Lutheran Church in America
Lutheran Church—Missouri Synod
United Methodist Church
Disciples of Christ
United Presbyterian Church, USA
Episcopal Church
Evangelical Covenant Church of America
Synagogue Council of America
Roman Catholic: U.S. Catholic Conference; American Catholic Bishops; National Federation of Priests' Councils
World Council of Churches

Chances are you'll be able to get help from your minister. And you should see a draft counselor.

CHAPTER 7
DOCUMENTING YOUR CO CLAIM

Whether you've decided to file for conscientious objector status or resist the draft, it's a good idea to put together evidence of what you believe and of your sincerity. If you're filing a claim with Selective Service, you'll need to show them that you qualify for CO status. Your local board won't look for proof of your claim; you have to provide it. If you resist the draft, a file of documents like supporting letters can help you to gain a lighter sentence if the government should prosecute you.

No matter which road you choose, the kinds of proof you'll need are similar. And you can begin to put together your documentation now, before you actually face your local board or a judge. The first part of this chapter gives ideas on evidence to support a CO claim or to use, if you have to, in court.

The second part of this chapter deals with the Special Form for Conscientious Objector (SSS Form 150) which was in use when inductions ended in 1972. No one knows whether this form will be used for a future draft, but understanding the questions on the 1972 form can help you in putting together a future CO application. This section will be useful primarily to people who plan to apply for CO status. But the questions on Form 150 could serve as a guide for planning a statement to give in court. So draft resisters may find this part useful also.

Your CO File

When you're putting together a CO claim, you should try to show four things:
- What you believe and why;
- How you came to believe it;
- Your sincerity;
- Actions that show you believe what you do.

You can show what you believe and why when you fill out Form 150 (or prepare your statement for the court). There's also a question on how you decided to be a CO, but your answer will be stronger if it's supported by other documents. Supporting letters can help to show that you're sincere. And when you show actions to support your claim, you're also showing that you really mean what you say.

Supporting Evidence

Don't worry if you can't support your claim with hundreds of pages of evidence. Many COs have been recognized even though they'd never been on a peace march, for instance. And too long a claim can be worse than one that's too short.

It's a good idea to start a file of proof that you're a CO. This doesn't have to be anything elaborate —even a shoe box will do. But it's important to keep it in a safe place where you can always find it. As you know from reading Chapter 3, if you do have to make a CO claim, you won't have much time to act. The more material you have ready, the better off you'll be in putting together your claim.

Of course, you shouldn't just put documents in your

file and never look at them again. Go through it now and then to see if there's anything that's gotten out of date, a supporting letter which you now feel you don't want to use, etc. When you talk with a draft counselor, take your file with you and go over it with your counselor to make sure it will really help you to present your case.

Except for your claim itself and your supporting letters, it's best not to submit original documents to your local board. For example, if you've written letters to the editor, copies of them will be good enough for your local board, and you'll run less risk of losing the originals.

Make copies of everything which you send to your local board. These copies can be part of your CO file, or you can keep them in a different file. The important thing is to have them, and to follow the other suggestions under "Protect Yourself. Follow These Suggested Rules," at the beginning of this *Handbook*.

Showing a History

Your local board can't deny your CO claim solely because you haven't been a CO for eight years, or ten years, or even ten months. But you'll increase your chances of being recognized if you can show that your claim isn't a new decision for you. Your supporting letters and your answers to the questions on SSS Form 150 will help.

But documentation will make your case much stronger. You can use your imagination here. In fact, you'll have to because each person is different. Have you ever been on a peace march? Or written letters to the editor, or anti-war poems or short stories? Have you spoken out against war in your school? What about membership in peace groups like the War Resisters League or the Fellowship of Reconciliation?

Some COs keep a kind of "diary" or notebook to keep track of actions which support their claims. Among items that you might include in such a notebook are participation in peace demonstrations, books or articles that you've read, movies, television shows, or plays you've seen, speakers you've heard, and other things which have helped to form your beliefs. You don't have to keep a diary, but it can be helpful in recalling things that happened months or even years ago.

If you decide to keep a diary, it's best to include too many things rather than too few. You can always cut out items when you're actually preparing your CO claim.

Most churches in this country support conscientious objectors. If your church does, or if it encourages its members to reject war, a statement from your minister (if you have one) and the official position of your church can help to show that you're sincere.

Were you raised to reject violence? Even if your family never told you about conscientious objection, the values you learned from them are part of you and may help to show a background that will convince your local board.

If you're not a member of a church, by the way, joining one of the "peace churches" won't help your CO claim. In fact, it might hurt because your local board might think you joined to avoid the draft. Your decision about whether to join a church, and which church to join, shiould be based on what you want to do, not on how it will affect your CO claim.

Documenting Your CO Claim—75

The CCCO Card

One way to show that your claim isn't something new is to register now with CCCO. CCCO will send you a "CO Registration Card" on request. If you fill the card out and return it, it will be kept on file for you. Then, when you need evidence to support your CO claim, CCCO will send you a statement showing the date you filed. The card itself will remain in CCCO's files for safekeeping.

The CCCO card is *not* an official application for conscientious objector status. It can help to make a stronger claim, but by itself it won't be enough. You'll need to file a formal CO claim with your local board, including the kinds of evidence which this chapter suggests.

In addition to CCCO, you can register with your local or national church. The CCCO Card has a space for this which you can fill out and return to your church. Or you can simply write to your church and tell them that you're a conscientious objector. Some churches have a formal national or regional registry. Others don't, but often local churches will acccept a registration letter or card.

What Have You Done?

One of the best ways to show your history and sincerity as a CO is to point to actions in your own life. You don't have to be a "political" person to do this. Many COs have never been on a peace march or joined a peace organization—though you may decide you want to do this.

Any action which shows that you live by your beliefs can be helpful. If you've worked for a community center after school or taken a lifesaving course at the

Red Cross, make a note of this or a copy of any documents (like a certificate received at the end of lifesaving training) and put it in your CO file. And, of course, note any actions like going on a demonstration.

Supporting Letters

An important part of your CO claim will be letters to show that you are sincere. You can get supporting letters from friends, family, teachers, ministers, or other people who know you and have some standing in the community. These people don't have to agree with your position. They do have to believe, and say, that you're sincere.

Most good CO claims include four to ten supporting letters. Fewer than four will make your claim seem weak—as if not very many people are ready to speak up for you. More than ten letters often will not be read, and your local board may think you are "protesting too much."

Your CO references will probably not have written a letter to a local board before. It's important for you to help them give you the best kind of support they can. CCCO has a memo on supporting letters which can help, but you should also tell your references what you expect. Here are some guidelines:

•Letters should be addressed to "Chairman, Local Board," even though you may not have a local board right now.

•A good supporting letter is first of all a character reference. Your reference doesn't have to know all the details of your claim, though it's good if he or she does. What your reference does have to know is that you're an honest person who means what you say.

•Supporting letters should tell how your reference

knows you, how long he or she has known you, and how closely.

• The letter should be as brief as possible. One page of single-spaced typing is a good length to try for.

• Typed letters and letters on letterhead are very impressive. But a neatly handwritten letter is okay, too. Since your local board will consider a lot of claims besides yours, it's important for your claim to be as easy as possible to read.

When you ask someone to write a supporting letter for you, you might want to give him or her a copy of your CO claim. That isn't necessary, though. If you haven't written up your claim, don't delay getting supporting letters until you've finished writing. What's most important is support for your honesty —not detailed knowledge of your claim.

Have your references send their letters to you, not to your local board (if you've been assigned one). When you've received your supporting letters, go over them to make sure that they support your claim and don't say things that contradict it. For instance, many well-meaning people say that a CO has been against war since he or she was a year old (or three years old or whatever). If you only claim to have been a CO for the last six months, a letter like that can hurt more than it helps. Return it to your reference and explain what the problem is. Chances are you'll be able to get a new and stronger letter.

Keep your supporting letters in your CO file, and look over them from time to time to make sure you still want to use them as part of your CO claim. If for some reason they seem out of date, you may want to ask for new letters.

Writing Your CO Claim

If you have to apply for CO status, you'll need to give a written statement of what you believe. No one knows what forms the draft system may use in the future. But SSS Form 150 (Special Form for Conscientious Objector), as used in the early 1970s, gives a good idea what questions will probably be used.

This form asks six questions, none of them easy. Although your induction will be postponed to allow your local board to consider your claim, you won't have very much time to complete your statement. It's a good idea to start working on your answers ahead of time. You'll find, too, that trying to write down your beliefs will help you to become more clear about what they are.

If you want to show that your beliefs are of long standing, one way to do it is to write a CO claim now, check it with your draft counselor, and then have it dated and notarized. You can then submit a copy, along with any updating you want to make, to your local board. Or if later on you find that you don't like the claim you wrote now, you can just keep it for your files.

You don't have to write a book in order to apply for CO status. In fact, the simpler your answers are, the better. If you have trouble writing, you might try talking about your beliefs with a friend or counselor who's taking notes. Or you might try talking about your beliefs to a tape recorder.

Good writing is very much like talking. You don't have to use big words or complicated sentences. If you try to write as you would talk, you'll probably find preparing your claim much easier. Once you have a first draft, you can polish it. The important thing is to get something on paper. When you've done this, you'll probably find that it was easier than you thought.

The Form 150 Questions

Question 1 on Form 150 asks: *Describe the beliefs which are the basis for your claim for classification as a conscientious objector.*

This question means just what it says. Your problem may be figuring out what it is you believe. Reread Chapter 5 of this *Handbook* to get an idea what kinds of beliefs the law recognizes. You'll note that your religious beliefs are the beliefs—whether you call them religious, moral, ethical, or a mixture —that lead you to be a conscientious objector.

Even though the question reads that way, it's not enough simply to state your beliefs. How do your beliefs lead you to be a conscientious objector? Remember that there are probably thousands, or even millions, of people who have beliefs much like yours but don't object to war. What makes you different? Your local board will want to know.

Question 2 asks: *Will your beliefs permit you to serve in a position in the armed forces where the use of weapons is not required? If not, why?*

If you're applying for 1-A-0 status, you should ask yourself whether you're sure you can be part of the military. If you're applying for 1-0 status, you should ask yourself why you're sure you can't be. Part V of this *Handbook* will be helpful to you whichever position you take. In nearly all cases, if your local board thinks you're sincere at all, they have to accept your sincerity in claiming to be 1-0 or 1-A-0. But if they have evidence that you qualify for the other status instead, they may try to give you a classification you don't want. A good answer to this question will help insure that you get the status you want. And in preparing your answer, you'll become more sure just what that status is.

Question 3 asks: *Explain how you acquired the beliefs which are the basis of your claim.*

Your CO file, if you have one, will be helpful in answering Question 3. This question gives you a chance to show your local board your background and convince them that you're sincere. You can include your childhood experiences, early religious training, books you have read, television shows or movies you have seen, people you have talked with, direct or indirect experience with the military—in fact, anything which will give your local board a good picture.

If you've ever been in the military (for instance, in Junior ROTC when you were in high school), it's a good idea to tell your local board about this and explain how your views have changed. They can't hold it against you unless you claim that you were a CO at the time you were in the military. Then they'll ask why your beliefs let you join then, but not now. And that would be a good question. Are your beliefs stronger now? Were you really a CO then? Did your time in the military actually turn you toward being a CO? It does for many people.

A good answer to Question 3 can make for a strong claim. You can organize your answer any way you want, but most COs find it easiest to start in childhood and work up to the present.

What Have You Done?

Questions 4, 5, and 6 are very similar. All are concerned with whether you have lived by your beliefs and how strongly you hold them. Some COs in the past have found them so much alike that they've answered the questions with one answer. Although this may confuse your local board, it's okay to do it if that's the best way for you.

Question 4 asks you to: *Explain what most clearly shows that your beliefs are deeply held.* For a discussion of "deeply held" beliefs, reread Chapter 5. You'll note that "deeply held" beliefs are the same as sincere beliefs—though your local board may think there is some difference. Anything which shows that you're sincere will also show that your beliefs are "deeply held." You might try to think of one action or incident that shows your beliefs more strongly than any other, but if you can't, the kind of information suggested for your CO file—such as membership in peace groups—can make a good answer to this question.

Question 5 asks: *Do your beliefs affect the way you live? Describe how your beliefs affect the type of work you will do to earn a living or the types of activity you participate in during nonworking hours.* Unless you already have your career planned—and chances are you don't—this will be a hard question to answer. As a minimum, you can tell your local board what you *won't* do. For instance, work in a defense plant or join the Army. If you have an idea what career you might want, this is the place to use it. The same goes for spare-time work that you want to do. What's most important is that you show how your values affect what you want to do. Even if you don't plan on a career in the peace movement (and almost nobody does), you can still show this. For instance, you may be interested in medicine or some other humanitarian field. Or you may have decided that you won't work for a company that underpays its employees. And so

Question 6 asks: *Describe any specific actions or incidents in your life that show you believe as you do.* This question is very much like Question 4. Again, the material in your CO file will be helpful in answering it. Along with the other two "lifestyle" questions, it's your best chance to give your own evidence that you're sincere.

Once You've Written Your Claim

When you've got a first or second draft of your claim, you should take it to a draft counselor and have him or her read it. Your draft counselor can't tell you what to say, but he or she may be able to help you improve the way you say it. And your counselor can spot weaknesses in your claim which you can then rewrite to make a stronger claim.

It's also a good idea to have someone who doesn't know the draft law look at your claim to make sure it's clear. Your local board is made up of ordinary citizens who aren't lawyers and have a lot of paperwork to get through. If you present a clear claim, you'll increase your chances of being recognized.

If you want to test your beliefs, you could show your claim to someone who doesn't agree with you and ask them to criticize your arguments. Your local board can't do this—they can only judge your sincerity and whether your claim fits under the law—but getting friendly criticism can help you become more confident in your stand. And it could help you to handle your personal appearance.

Statements for Court

Even if you're applying for CO status, you don't

have to follow Form 150 exactly. It's best to do this, of course, but COs have made good claims by combining their answers to the Form 150 questions into one statement. This is even more possible if you're preparing a statement for a judge.

Questions 1 and 3 on Form 150 are a good outline of what your court statement might cover. If you've refused to register, you'll need to say why you weren't willing to follow the legal procedure. If you've refused induction, you'll need to explain why you did this. But by following the suggestions in this chapter, you'll be able to present a statement which may move the judge to sentence you to a shorter jail term or even probation.

Making a statement to the judge is *not* the same as presenting a defense. In fact, a statement of your reasons for breaking the law might actually hurt some defenses. So in most cases you'll want to reserve your statement for use when the judge is considering your sentence. It's best, in any case, to consult your lawyer about any statement you plan to make in court.

CHAPTER 8
ALTERNATIVE SERVICE

If your local board places you in Class 1-0, chances are you'll be called for "civilian work in lieu of induction," or, as it's usually known, alternative service. As you've seen in Chapter 3, you can only apply for CO status after you've been called for induction. Since 1-0 objectors are supposed to be called for alternative service when they would have been called for induction, you can see that, unless you qualify for some other deferment—or fail the Armed Forces physical examination—Selective Service will call you for alternative service as soon as they can after you've been granted CO status.

If you're applying for another deferment or exemption, you may want to appeal your 1-0 classification and try to get Selective Service to grant your deferment claim. You'll find details on appeal procedures in Chapter 3. An appeal from Class 1-0 to a lower classification wouldn't change your 1-0 classification. If your appeal fails, you should be returned to Class 1-0. To protect yourself against Selective Service mistakes, you can write a note with your appeal explaining that you are not dropping your CO claim but merely seeking another, lower classification that you feel you qualify for.

The New Proposal

In January, 1981, draft officials completed a proposal for an entire new alternative service program. Regulations which spell out more of the proposal were proposed in June, 1982. Because neither the proposal nor the regulations were final as this *Handbook* went to press, you shouldn't rely on this chapter. Check with CCCO or your draft counselor for the latest information.

Even though the new proposal isn't final, it shows how draft officials are thinking about the civilian work program. That's important for you to know.

Selective Service's plan would create a special alternative service office within the draft system. This new office would work with the Federal Emergency Management Agency (FEMA), which is also responsible for civil defense and coordinating emergency mobilization. The Director of Selective Service would create a computerized job bank. He or she would also set up priorities to determine which jobs you might be assigned to.

You wouldn't have much chance to choose your own job under this system. If you found a job which qualified as alternative service, you might be able to persuade Selective Service to approve it. But the new rules would allow the Director to send you to a job of his or her choice without regard to your choices. Selective Service would investigate grievances which you had against an employer, so if you were stuck in a bad job you might be able to get a job change or a change in your working conditions. But if draft officials determined that you hadn't been working satisfactorily, they could refuse to give you credit for work which you'd already done.

The purpose of this more centralized system, at

least in part, would be to fill in gaps left when civilian employees were drafted or enlisted into the military. COs would be closely integrated into an overall "mobilization plan"—in effect, they might be part of the war effort. This would be similar to the system used in England during World War II, when many COs were used to fill gaps left by the draft. Many English COs objected to this system, and, under English law, they could apply for and receive exemption from all work. Selective Service's proposal wouldn't allow anyone to be exempt from all work.

You'll have to decide for yourself whether a system like this would be okay for you to take part in. But you don't have to decide now. The new proposal is just that: a proposal. If and when inductions begin again, this new proposal could be long forgotten, replaced by another which is better—or worse.

The Alternative Service Requirement

Section 6(j) of the Military Selective Service Act requires that COs who oppose all military duty are to serve two years of civilian work "in lieu of induction." This is the basic alternative service requirement. The details, such as what kinds of jobs qualify, are left up to the President and the Director of Selective Service.

In the past, work with government agencies, hospitals, and non-profit groups like the Mennonite Central Committee have been used as alternative service. It's possible that these kinds of jobs will be acceptable again. It's also possible that Selective Service will accept jobs with profit-making companies. In fact, in the early 1970s, they revised the draft rules to permit this.

One new feature of the proposed regulations is called "orientation." Selective Service hasn't given any details on orientation, but it's possible that draft officials will try to set up "training camps," or special work camps for COs. No one knows. If draft officials do try to set up camps, though, they'd probably have to fight a lawsuit. Work camps were actually used for COs during World War II, and, when Congress created a new alternative service program in 1951, the report of the committee which wrote the 1951 draft law said that Congress opposed creating new work camps. This would give good legal grounds for arguing against any new work camps.

No one knows what may happen. All that we know, as this *Handbook* goes to press, is that COs who would have been called for induction will be called for two years alternative service. And we can be pretty sure that it won't be under the old rules.

Physical Examination

One rule which is changed drastically under the new rules is the physical examination requirement. In the past, COs could skip their physical examinations if they wished, and then they would simply be considered acceptable for alternative service.

Under the new rules, if they become final, COs would be called for a physical examination just like everyone else. A CO couldn't skip the examination. But, of course, he might fail it and avoid having to do alternative service at all.

Whatever becomes of the new rules, it's a good idea to take the physical. You may fail it, and be saved from two years of enforced work. And even if you don't fail it, you'll learn from it a bit more about what you're objecting to.

What You Can Do Now

As you can see, the alternative service program wasn't really set up at the time this *Handbook* went to press. What can you do now about alternative service? It's hard to say.

One point to think about is whether you want to be part of alternative service at all. Keep in mind that refusing to perform alternative service is a violation of the draft law, with the same penalties as refusing induction or refusing to register. But you may feel that alternative service is too much a part of the war effort to satisfy your conscience. In the past, many COs took this position. They left their jobs, or, in World War II, walked out of the work camps where they were assigned.

You may decide that you want to perform two years of alternative service. Many COs took this position in the past. Even some who failed their physical examinations went ahead and did two years of service voluntarily.

Or you may find that you can't make this decision without knowing more about the program—information which isn't available yet. Whether you accept alternative service or not is a decision which you can safely put off until you need to make it. But you may want to think about it now.

Another decision, though, is important now. That's your decision about the kind of work you might want to do as alternative service. You can think about this even though you don't know what kinds of work will be accepted, because the kinds of work you prefer is *your* decision. If you have an idea of what kind of work you prefer to do—and would be better at—you'll have a better chance of getting a good alternative service job if and when you need one. The reason is simple:

chances are you won't have much time to locate a job or convince Selective Service that you should work in your chosen field. If you don't have a chosen field, chances are that draft officials will place you where the "needs of the nation" dictate.

What kind of work would fit with your values? Would you be willing to work for the government? For a non-profit service agency? What do *you* think are the most important problems for you to work on? By asking yourself questions like these, you'll have a better idea where you stand on alternative service, and you may become more clear about the kind of work you'd like to do, draft or no draft.

Decisions about alternative service are like the other decisions mentioned in this *Handbook*. Selective Service can decide if you, or a job you propose, qualify under their rules. But only you can decide what you believe and what you'd like to do.

PART III

THINKING ABOUT WAR RESISTANCE

A NOTE TO THE READER

Most of the chapters in this *Handbook* give CCCO's best understanding of the draft law, resistance, and the other issues they talk about. That isn't true of the next five chapters. In this Part of the *Handbook*, you'll find only my own ideas and opinions.

These chapters deal with issues that are important to you if you want to understand war and think about where you stand on it. But you don't have to agree with what's said in them to qualify as a conscientious objector.

You can even skip them and still know how to make a good conscientious objector claim. I hope you won't. I learned a lot in writing them, and I think you can learn from reading them.

I don't have a clear stand on everything covered in these chapters. But I've tried to present the issues as clearly as I could. I hope you'll find these chapters helpful.

—R.A.S.

CHAPTER 9
SOME THOUGHTS ON WAR

Historians, politicians, sociologists, psychologists, anthropologists, military officers, pacifists, and other citizens have studied war almost since the beginning of civilization. They have written hundreds of books, articles, and reports of studies. They have argued for and against war, traced it to different causes, and suggested many different ways to end it.

Yet few people even agree on what war is. Does the Cold War count as war? Does there have to be a declaration of war? If so, what was Vietnam where there was no declaration? What was Korea, which was called a "police action"? Is guerilla warfare really war, or do we need a new name for it?

The courts haven't really ruled on what war means as a matter of law. Among the cases on conscientious objection are many on force and violence which distinguish the use of force from war. But there is no case which *defines* war. A state court in Virginia ruled in the late 1960s that, for life insurance purposes, the Vietnam conflict was a war. Even that court, though, didn't try to define war.

Historians don't even always agree on when wars begin. World War I began on a known and agreed date (August 4, 1914). But some historians think that World War II began when the Japanese invaded

Manchuria in 1932. Others think it began with Hitler's invasion of Poland in 1939. Still others think that the Far East wars of 1932-1941 and the European war of 1939-1941 were separate wars, and the World War didn't begin until the Japanese bombed Pearl Harbor in 1941.

A Definition of War

This chapter won't try to resolve these disputes. Instead, it will define war as armed conflict between two or more countries or between rival military forces within one country. This means that the Battle of Waterloo was part of a war, as were the Battle of Verdun in 1916 and the Siege of Dien Bien Phu in 1954. Guerilla warfare comes under this definition. World Wars I and II, Korea, Vietnam, and Afghanistan, among others, are wars by this definition.

In order for war to be taking place, there needn't be a declaration of war. A declaration of war is a diplomatic device, and it has legal effects both internationally and within the country that has declared war. (For instance, parts of the U.S. draft law don't apply after a declaration of war.) But few wars today are formally declared. Vietnam was not. Afghanistan was not. The Iran-Iraq war of the early 1980s was not. And so on.

The Cold War isn't a war by this chapter's definition. It is "geopolitics," as discussed in Chapter 2. The military forces of the U.S. and the Soviet Union are competing all the time for better strategic position. They do this by buying new weapons, moving their forces around, preparing strategic plans, and by actual shows of force like sending an aircraft carrier to the Persian Gulf. But there has been no direct armed conflict between the two countries since 1919. There has only been the threat of war—and of total destruction, as you'll see in the next chapter.

War and the Arms Race

Many historians believe that arms races in themselves don't cause wars. This may surprise you. Common sense tells you that when two countries mistrust each other and arm against each other, they're more likely to fight. But the argument isn't as weak as it sounds. The causes of any particular war are many, and it's hard to know which is most important. And the causes of war itself—the explanation of why people fight—may not even include the arms race. It may be that people make weapons because they're willing to fight—not that people are willing to fight because they make weapons.

Still, arms races increase world tensions. This could make war more likely. And by increasing the firepower on both sides, an arms race makes a war, if it comes, larger and more terrible. But the relationship between war and the arms race is pretty complex.

There's a good argument, for instance, that war causes the arms race, not the reverse. Military planners base much of their thinking on what wars they believe are likely. The arms race may be called "defense" or "a necessary response to imperialist aggression," or whatever. In fact, it is a preparation for war. Types of weapons, size of armies, placement of troops, etc., are determined mainly by plans for future wars.

An example of this is U.S. war plans. In the early

1960s, Pentagon planners tried to be prepared for two wars—one in Europe and one in another part of the world. Then, under the Nixon administration, they were directed to plan for 1½ wars—a large one in Europe and a small one somewhere else. Now they are prepared for a large war in Europe and a "crisis" in another part of the world. Each of these predictions means a different size army, different weapons, and different strategies. And the U.S. is armed, as most other nations are, because it accepts war as one way of settling international disputes or gaining power.

Whether war causes the arms race, or the arms race causes war, there's no doubt that, when the shooting starts, the arms race speeds up. Both sides arm themselves as heavily as they can, and both try to develop new weapons quickly, before their opponents do.

Between 1870 and 1914, for instance, there was no war in Europe. Few new weapons were developed. During World War I, however, literally hundreds of new weapons were made and tried. Many are now standard in warfare: the tank, the flamethrower, the airplane, aerial bombing, and the trench mortar, among others. Others are against the "laws of war," but could still be used in a future war. Poison gas was outlawed right after the 1914-1918 war, but many countries have huge stocks of gas like that used in World War I, and worse gas, such as the U.S. military's nerve gas.

The Structure of the Military

A modern army fights what is called "drilled warfare." This name comes from the use of drill in training troops. The basic structure of armies hasn't changed much since Roman times. At the top of the army is a supreme commander who sets overall strategy. Below the commander is a "chain of command," made up of lower-ranking officers. The army is built up from small units, each under the command of a low-ranking officer (like a lieutenant) or a high-ranking enlisted person (like a sergeant). Several of these small units make up a larger unit, and several of these larger units make up a still larger unit, and so on up the chain of command.

The reason for all this dividing up is to make military units interchangeable, like machine parts. In combat, a soldier may be killed or wounded. A unit may have too many killed and wounded and become "exhausted." Or the strain of fighting may make it less "combat-effective." One unit must be able to replace another that can no longer fight. And one soldier must be able to replace another who is killed, wounded, or battle-weary. So the military is divided into standard parts. Military jobs are standard, so that anybody can learn them.

Although a modern army may draw its officers from all walks of life, the division between officers (higher-ranking soldiers who command and plan strategy) and enlisted persons (lower-ranking soldiers under the command of officers) goes back to early armies in which the lower-ranking soldiers were drawn from the lower ranks of society and the officers were drawn from the nobility. Many military customs like separate clubs for officers also have their roots in earlier armies. This makes the command structure into a kind of class structure.

The military hierarchy makes it very difficult for a low-ranking soldier to challenge unreasonable orders or abuses of power. And it means that in many cases enlisted soldiers run far greater risks than officers. But this isn't always so. In Vietnam, for instance, 2nd

Lieutenants commanding combat units had a very high casualty rate. And in the World War I British army, an officer in the front lines had an average life expectancy of *six weeks;* an enlisted man might expect to live for ten weeks.

The military structure is supposed to help officers in planning operations. Instead of moving one soldier here and another there, strategists can move entire units. In most armies, the local commander can choose tactics that suit conditions like weather, terrain, etc. On paper, this makes for efficient operations. It doesn't, of course, always work that way in practice. Some of the reasons why this happens will be found under ''Combat,'' below.

The Weapons of War

Throughout history, military forces have used whatever weapons they had, and they have tried to develop new weapons to gain an advantage over their opponents. The result, today, is that armies have a choice of thousands of different weapons and tactics.

Most modern weapons are designed to destroy and kill people at a distance. Examples would be artillery, guided missiles, and the rifle. Some weapons kill automatically, without a human being to fire them. During the Indochina War, for instance, American forces used electronic weapons (like very sophisticated minefields) which would fire if anyone crossed certain parts of the jungle. And some weapons, called ''smart'' weapons, track their targets using built-in controls like heat-seeking devices and computers. Many ''smart'' weapons have a 90% chance of hitting their targets.

Not all modern weapons are designed to kill. Anti-personnel weapons, as military planners call them, are designed to disable and maim the enemy as well as kill. One weapon used during the Vietnam War sprayed plastic pellets when it exploded. These transparent bullets would wound anyone within range, and they would be very difficult to remove. The idea was to tie up enemy hospitals with long and complicated surgery.

Weapons like napalm (a compound which burns and sticks to human flesh), the automatic battlefield, and anti-personnel explosives do not distinguish between enemy soldiers and civilians. Neither do bombs dropped from airplanes. That is why, in many modern wars, there are far more civilian than military casualties. The last major war where this was not true, in fact, was World War I.

Some people think that weapons like these—and others which haven't yet been used, like nerve gas—have made even modern "conventional" (non-nuclear) war unjustified. Many who hold these views might have fought in past wars, but would not fight today. Yet even in past wars, as far back as ancient times, technology was used for terrible destruction. Towns were burned using weapons similar to napalm. Wells were poisoned. Some ancient armies even used a kind of poison gas. Has anything really changed? You'll have to decide this question for yourself.

In any case, there's no doubt that modern war is far more destructive than the wars of, say, the 1700s. This is because of modern weapons, but it is also because tactics have changed and become more ruthless. For more on this, see the sections on "Total War" and "Guerilla War," below.

The Laws of War

Even among people who thought some wars were justified, there have been many attempts to control the destruction which war causes. The "laws of war" cover everything from treatment of wounded and prisoners to which weapons can lawfully be used.

The "laws of war," however, aren't quite like the laws which you follow every day—for example, traffic laws or laws against robbery. They are based on agreements among the nations of the world, called "conventions," and on precedents like the Nuremberg War Crimes Trials. There isn't any real way to enforce them, and there's no court that can order a country, say, to stop using poison gas.

This means that countries at war don't always follow the laws of war. And sometimes it means that the laws of war don't make a great deal of sense. For instance, an international convention outlaws the use of poison gas. No convention outlaws the machine gun. Yet the machine gun has been used far more than poison gas, and it has killed far more people.

If you're a conscientious objector, you probably think that war itself is so evil that no "laws of war" can make it better. In many ways that's true. But without the "laws of war," prisoners might still be slaughtered, as they were in ancient wars. There might be no Red Cross to help the wounded. And nations which have, say, nerve gas might be quicker to use it.

For people in the military, the "laws of war" can be very important. A U.S. military member has a legal right to refuse an order that violates international conventions. Most soldiers don't do this becacuse they don't know they can or because they're afraid of what might happen to them. But if you decide to go into the military and find that you're given orders against your conscience, you may be able to refuse the orders. You shouldn't, of course, refuse any order until you've talked with CCCO or a military counselor.

The Language of War

War has its own strange language. If you want to get an idea what happened in a battle or a war, or if you just want to get an idea what you're objecting to, you must translate this language into ordinary speech.

Two simple rules of thumb will help: Most of us talk about war in ways that keep us from seeing it as it really is. Politicians and military planners talk about it in a way that keeps the public from seeing what is happening. You can probably pick out examples from the daily newspaper, but here are three.

Military officers often talk about "mopping up." This is another way of saying, "Searching a captured area for enemy survivors and killing them or taking them prisoner." It doesn't sound quite as good the second way, but that's a better description of what actually happens.

A related example is the use of *jargon*. In Washington this is sometimes called "Pentagonese." Jargon not only tries to fool the public, but often fools everyone, including other military planners, because it's so hard to understand. A "shortfall," discussed in Chapter 2, is jargon. A worse example comes from the Vietnam era. In the late 1960s and early 1970s, American bombers were dropping tons of explosives on North Vietnam. These bombing raids were called "protective reaction strikes." If this jargon means anything—and it's not clear that it does—it means simply that the U.S. Air Force attacked North Vietnam with bombs. But by saying this in jargon, the

Pentagon gave people the idea that we were really only defending ourselves.

A more subtle example is the way historians talk about battles. Many of them talk as though generals did all the fighting. A historian may say, "Field Marshall Petain held the Verdun front in 1916 when Gen. Falkenhayn attacked it." This is obviously not true. Neither general did any such thing. Falkenhayn was in Germany giving orders, hundreds of miles from Verdun. Petain was miles behind the front lines. Hundreds of thousands of ordinary soldiers did the fighting at Verdun. And nearly a million of them died.

Whenever you read about a war, try to keep this kind of thing in mind, and you'll have a better idea what's really going on.

Total War

Modern war is often called "total war." Total war is often thought to be new in this century, but in many ways it isn't. Ancient wars, for instance, were often total in the sense that the loser's cities and crops were destroyed, the men slaughtered, and the women and children taken captive.

But today's total war is so different from past wars that it is a new development. Before the mid-19th Century, armies were small, and most wars were fought on battlefields away from the civilian population. A country that went to war didn't put all its industry to work making war supplies and ammunition, as happens today. There was no such thing as bombing of cities, though cities were often beseiged and even destroyed.

All this began to change with the American Civil War. In that war, armies—and casualties—were huge by the standards of past wars. The railroad made troop movements easier and more rapid than they had ever been before. The telegraph made for fast communication. Even the weapons used were rifles that shot modern-style bullets, rather than muskets which shot lead balls as in earlier wars.

Most important, the Civil War saw the first use of a direct attack against the enemy's population rather than the enemy's army. For many people, this is what makes modern war different from past wars. Gen. William Tecumseh Sherman of the Union Army believed that the best way to defeat the Confederacy was to destroy its economy and its "will to fight." His troops first occupied and destroyed Atlanta—then, as now, a major trade center. They then marched in a line several miles wide from Atlanta to the Georgia coast, burning crops, killing those who resisted them, and destroying property as they went. This "March to the Sea" split the Confederacy and ruined its economy, just as Sherman had predicted. It was a total war tactic.

Direct attacks against civilians are forbidden by the laws of war, but they are common in modern war. The British blockaded German shipping in World War I and caused great hardship and starvation among the civilian population. The Allies bombed German cities in World War II, and the Germans bombed Great Britain. All these are total war tactics.

Even a "limited" modern war can become a total war, and usually does. In 1870, Prussian troops invaded France in a "limited" action. The advancing troops killed many civilians and destroyed much property. They surrounded Paris and tried to starve the population into surrender. The Siege of Paris was a total war tactic even in a "limited" war.

Guerilla War

Guerilla warfare got its name from the Spanish armed resistance to Napoleon's armies. Guerillas are soldiers who live among the civilian population, usually supported by them (willingly or not), and operate by small, fast attacks against "conventional" forces and by sabotage. A conventional army usually has trouble defeating a guerilla force because guerilla soldiers disappear into the population when they aren't fighting.

Because it's often hard to tell the soldiers from the civilians—or, as in Vietnam, impossible—war against guerilla forces (called "counter insurgency warfare") doesn't involve battles as we usually understand them. A counter insurgency force attacks not only the guerilla forces, but the population which supports them. So, for instance, crops were destroyed in Vietnam to try to cut off the guerillas' food supplies. Jungles were "defoliated" (sprayed with a powerful weed killer) to make it harder for the guerillas to hide. Entire villages were evacuated and destroyed. And so on. The same kinds of tactics have been used by Soviet armies in Afghanistan, the Rhodesian army before majority rule in that country, and the South African army.

This isn't surprising. Many military experts think that one guerilla can defeat as many as ten conventional soldiers by using stealth, harassment, and civilian support. Many others think that fighting guerillas will be the main work of Western armies in the future. This is true not only of people in the peace movement, who oppose counter insurgency war, but of military thinkers who support it.

Combat

The reason for nearly everything that armies do —from training to medical services to the design of boots—is combat. If an army cannot fight when the shooting starts, it will fail in its main mission.

This seems clear enough. And it seems clear enough what combat is. It is actual armed conflict. An army's object in combat is to kill, wound, or capture enemy soldiers and take over enemy territory and positions without losing more of its own soldiers than it has to. Military thinkers argue about whether a winning army must destroy the other army, convince the other side's generals that they can't win, or destroy the other side's ability to go on by destroying factories and killing civilians. In modern total war, this kind of argument means less than it once did. Modern armies try to do all three.

Armies today fight, in many ways, as they have for centuries. They follow a strategy (overall plan) using tactics (methods of fighting) based on conditions where they are fighting and the weapons they are using. Modern armies are said to fight in three "dimensions:" land, sea, and air. On land, they use artillery to shock and kill the enemy from a distance. They use tanks to move into good positions more quickly than the enemy and to destroy communications and defenses. They use infantry (foot soldiers) to "secure" positions and go places where tanks can't. Airplanes attack the enemy's soldiers or the enemy's cities. Ships can cut off the enemy's supplies or attack the enemy from a distance (for instance, by shelling a beach).

The "art of war" has become very complex and destructive. But the aim of combat hasn't changed very much over the years. Combat consists of killing and destroying according to a plan, and avoiding being killed and destroyed at the same time. The army with the best plan often wins—but not always.

Combat is unpredictable. People and units aren't really interchangeable. Combat is noisy, deadly, dirty, and frightening. No matter how well-trained a soldier is, he or she may break under the strain. Or something may go wrong—a tank may fail to start, or soldiers may be killed by their own side's fire. Or even a well-trained soldier may go berserk and kill anyone in sight.

This doesn't happen often because soldiers usually follow orders. In fact, you could say that, while combat is violent, soldiers, for the most part, are not. They're ordinary people in a terrible situation. It's important to remember this as you're thinking about war. Combat soldiers are probably about your age. Before they were trained to fight, they were very much like you. They still are. Military training, where actions like firing a gun are repeated until they become automatic, makes them able to kill. And in combat, they do things which they wouldn't do on the street.

Combat soldiers are following orders. They do this because they're afraid of punishment and humiliation in front of their fellow soldiers. They do it because it's automatic after their training. And they do it because combat is one of the most frightening situations a person can be in. Most people will defend themselves if they're threatened. That's even more true when they've gone through military training.

But a soldier's training doesn't make him or her inhuman. One of the worst costs of war is the thousands of soldiers who have been in combat and survived—and now have to live with the memory of what they saw and what they were forced to do. Many find it very hard, indeed.

The Costs of War

War has killed millions of people, soldiers and civilians alike. You'll find some casualty figures in the next chapter. But figures like these are hard to imagine. Here are two passages which give an idea of the human cost of war. The first is from World War I:

> One of the first things that struck troops fresh to the Verdun battlefield was the fearful stench of putrefaction [rotting corpses]. ... It was safe[st] to wrap the dead up in a canvas and simply roll them over the parapet [of a trench] into the largest shell-hole in the vicinity. ... [One gully filled with corpses] was enfiladed [fired upon from the side] by a German machine gun at each end, which exacted a heavy toll. Day after day the German [heavy artillery] pounded the corpses in this gully. ... [One writer who was at the battle described this]: "Shells disinter the bodies, then reinter them, chop them to pieces, play with them as a cat plays with a mouse."

And from World War II:

> Just before noon a single 8-inch shell from a long-range German gun came snoring overhead to bury itself in the center of the bivouac area.
> The explosion seemed of unprecedented violence. I was standing some distance from the burst and as the concussion buffeted me I saw a massive cone of mud spring full blown, like an instant genie, out of the sodden ground. A hot wind filled my nostrils. Childlike, I screwed my eyes tight shut against this

terror and willed my body not to run.

When I looked out into the world it was to see a black-rimmed crater where the regimental aid post had stood short seconds earlier. There remained only some meaningless fragments of the equipment which, alone in war's panoply, is intended to heal rather than destroy. There remained only bloodied fragments of Charlie Krakauer, of the medical sergeant and half a dozen orderlies and stretcher-bearers.

Measured in dollars, war and preparing for war cost more than any other single human activity. The nations of the world now spend over half a trillion dollars each year on armies and weapons.

Economic and human costs are not the only ones. War damages the environment. This is clear when we speak of nuclear war, but conventional wars of the past have also done immense harm. In Vietnam, as you've seen above, jungles were "defoliated," crops were destroyed, and cities were bombed. World War II left much of Europe in ruins, particularly in Germany, but also in other countries. Not only crops and forests, but priceless buildings have been destroyed by shelling and bombing. Entire towns are often leveled by tanks and artillery.

Militarism

One side-effect of war and preparing for war is *militarism*. Sidney B. Fay, a well-known expert on the origins of World War I, gave two definitions of militarism: "First, the dangerous and burdensome mechanism of great standing armies and large navies, with the attendant evils of espionage, suspicion, fear, and hatred. Second, the existence of a powerful class of military and naval officers ... who tend to dominate, especially at a time of political crisis, over the civilian authorities." Another definition says that militarism is the love of military things—like uniforms, weapons, and parades—for themselves. A fourth says that militarism is the belief that military force can solve all or most of the problems which a nation has in its foreign policy.

As you can imagine, militarism can often be dangerous. Many people in the U.S., for instance, believe that the solution to shortages of oil and raw materials is to increase U.S. military strength. Whether or not this is true, it probably increases the chances of war. So does the belief that military values are "strong," and therefore good, and peaceful values are "weak," and therefore bad.

The Causes of War

Thinkers over the centuries have argued about the cause of war. Some anthropologists believe that humans have a "killer instinct" which leads them to make war. Marxists and many others hold that war is caused by a need for capitalist countries to expand their markets and control resources. Some people think that war is caused by misunderstandings that result because the people on both sides don't know each other well enough. Others argue that wars happen because each nation acts like a law unto itself in foreign affairs.

All of these ideas have some basis, and all have some flaws. The "killer instinct," for instance, hasn't been proved. In fact, much of the evidence is the other way. And even if there were a "killer instinct," that wouldn't explain how a particular war, like World War II, began.

Sidney B. Fay said that we must separate the immediate causes of war from its underlying causes. This is a good place to begin in trying to understand the causes of war. When you read about a war in history, you can learn much by trying to see how that particular war got started. Was it because of blunders by diplomats? Attacks by one nation on another? Or what?

At the same time, this won't tell you much about why there are wars at all. And that's an important —and much harder—question. You can study it for years and still not really know. But you can learn a lot by trying, if you're interested.

One thing is clear. Whatever causes war, there wouldn't be any wars at all if people refused to fight. And after all is said and done, that's the main issue for you: Will you fight or not? You can decide this without knowing the causes of any war. You're the only expert on this question.

CHAPTER 10
YOU AND NUCLEAR WAR

Wars have always been deadly. In the seventeenth century, eight million people died in Germany alone during the Thirty Years War (1618-1648). The American Civil War killed 529,000 on both sides; World War I, ten million; World War II, 38 million.

But worst of all for the world of today were the deaths of 100,000 in one brief moment at Hiroshima.

The Hiroshima bombing marked the beginning of the atomic age in warfare. Many people think that it changed the rules of war for all time. Today war could mean the end, not just of one nation or of civilization, but of humanity itself. That has never been true before.

What Nuclear War Would Do

No one knows what a full-scale nuclear war would be like. Some experts believe that 100-170 million Americans would die in such a conflict. Survivors would have little or no food and would face great danger from radiation. Nuclear fallout might cover much of the country. And, as we are learning today, those who lived through a nuclear war might die of cancer years later and have stillborn or deformed children.

Nuclear war would not only destroy cities and people. It would poison the environment—perhaps beyond repair. Even a small amount of radiation can be dangerous. A 450-rem* dose is fatal to half of those who are exposed to it. A nuclear war would release millions—perhaps billions—of rem into the air. Could the earth, air, and water absorb so much radiation and still support life? Even the experts cannot say, but many believe they could not.

In 1976, the United States had a nuclear arsenal equal to 8,000 million tons of dynamite. The rest of the world had about as much. The weapons in the U.S. arsenal alone were enough to kill every person on earth *twelve times over.*

How Large Is the Bomb?

Figures like these don't give much idea what a nuclear attack would really be like. It's hard even to understand how big today's nuclear warheads are. But you can get an idea by thinking of tons of TNT. A conventional bomb has the power of ½ ton of TNT. The largest conventional bomb has the power of 10 tons of TNT.

The explosive power of nuclear weapons is measured in thousands or millions of tons of TNT power. For instance, a small nuclear bomb has the power of 10 kilotons, or 10,000 tons of TNT. The Hiroshima bomb had the power of 10,000-20,000 tons of TNT.

Even a small modern Inter-Continental Ballistic Missile (ICBM), however, makes the Hiroshima bomb

---

*A "rem" (roentgen equivalent, manual) is a unit for measuring radiation. It is equal in effect to one roentgen of X-ray radiation.

look tiny. Polaris and Minuteman missiles carry warheads with the power of 1-2 megatons of TNT. That is 1,000,000-2,000,000 tons of TNT power.

To give yourself an idea how large this really is, you can imagine a very long freight train. In order to hold one megaton of TNT, the train would have to be made up of 300 box cars. At full speed, the train would take six hours to pass as you watched it go by.

An H-Bomb in Manhattan

Even a one-megaton bomb is not very large for a nuclear warhead. Some land-based missiles and bombs carried in aircraft are 15-25 megatons in size, or 100 times the size of the Hiroshima bomb. Nuclear bombs this large—along with thousands of "smaller" bombs—could be used against Soviet and American cities in a nuclear war.

What would happen if a 20-megaton bomb fell in midtown Manhattan? One study describes the devastation that such a bomb would cause.

First, the sky would fill with a bluish-white fireball whose heat at the center would be nearly that of the sun itself. This fireball would expand until it was four miles wide. "To the west it spans the Hudson River; to the east it reaches across the river to Queens. Times Square, Rockefeller Center, big ocean liners, Central Park, the United Nations are instantly incinerated."

Following the fireball would come a pressure wave traveling at speeds many times that of sound. It would spread from the center of the explosion, crushing everything in its path until it slowly lost its force. Winds, some at thousands of miles per hour, would follow the pressure wave and destroy anything that might be left standing.

This wind, rushing outward, would create a vacuum at the center of the city. When the outward wind had lost its force, the vacuum at the center would trigger a reverse windstorm. The reverse winds would rush back to the center of the city, fanning any flames which the first explosion had started—whether from the explosion itself or from broken gas mains, short circuits, upset stoves, or other causes. The fire department could not cope with such fires, for there might be more than a million separate fires to begin with. There would be no water, and most fire fighters would be dead or badly burned. The fires would condense into a firestorm which, like a fire in a fireplace, would suck in air from around its edges, creating even more hurricane-force winds.

Six million people would die either instantly or within a few days.

Even far from "ground zero" (the center of the blast) there would be immense damage. At twenty-seven miles from ground zero, a person might receive third-degree burns; at thirty-two miles, second-degree burns; at forty-five miles, first-degree burns. Those with second- and third-degree burns would probably also die.

These would be only the first effects of the blast. Since all medical facilities would be crippled, those who somehow survived the explosion might die slowly and painfully over the next few weeks. If they did not die then, exposure to radiation might bring on cancer. And their unborn children might be deformed or even dead at birth.

"Nuclear Strategy"

Many people, including many military officers, believe that destruction like this makes large-scale war too dangerous to risk. Rear Admiral Gene LaRocque (U.S. Navy, Ret.) put it this way:

> There is no defense. We can't defend ourselves against Soviet missiles, and the Russians can't defend themselves against our missiles. There's nowhere to hide.

Lord Mountbatten, who fought in World Wars I and II, said:

> As a military man who has given half a century of active service I say in all sincerity that the nuclear arms race has no military purpose. Wars cannot be fought with nuclear weapons.

Not only would nuclear war be destructive, it wouldn't accomplish anything. It would be what military theorists call "absolute war"—war which can only destroy, not gain any political end.

But "nuclear strategists" don't talk much about what would happen if there were a nuclear war. Both sides in the arms race believe in "deterrence" because they believe that it prevents war from happening. The idea of "deterrence" seems simple: If you have enough weapons, you can frighten your opponents so that they won't use their weapons. So, for instance, if U.S. planners think the Soviets have a bomb that would destroy U.S. missiles, the U.S. will try to build missiles that the Soviet bomb couldn't destroy. They will do this because they think that if they don't they will lose their "deterrent" and be attacked. A nation feels that it will lose its "deterrent" if the other side gets an "advantage" in the arms race.

The trouble with this idea, according to its critics, is

that it doesn't work. When each side can destroy the other ten times over, does "advantage" have any meaning? For example, even if all U.S. land-based guided missiles were destroyed in a surprise attack, the U.S. could still destroy most Soviet cities using missiles mounted on submarines. Who has the "advantage" here? *Both* sides would suffer immense destruction. Would there be a winner in such an exchange of missiles? Even for those who support "deterrence," it's hard to say.

"Deterrence" is a strange idea—and a new one in military history. Before there were nuclear weapons, most countries built weapons with the idea that they might be used. Now, many weapons are built with the idea that they *won't* be used, except to frighten the other side. But the more weapons there are, and the more countries that have them, the more dangerous the world is. The arms race increases tensions. And it doesn't prevent wars like Vietnam and Afghanistan.

Meanwhile, say its critics, the arms race costs a great deal of money. It makes the world more dangerous. New computers and other "automatic retaliation" devices have made war by accident more and more likely. In 1979, for instance, U.S. forces were alerted for nuclear war four times. All four alerts were caused by computer malfunctions.

Nuclear "deterrence," the critics say, is too dangerous to go on. The only safe alternative is peace.

Nuclear Pacifism

Many people have come to agree with LaRocque and Mountbatten about nuclear war. They have begun to work for disarmament. Some have become "nuclear pacifists," who believe that use of nuclear weapons can never be justified. Or they may have rejected all wars—for instance, because they believe a large conventional war would soon become a nuclear holocaust.

All three groups of people agree on one thing: nuclear war and nuclear weapons are the greatest danger we have ever faced. The arms race, they say, is more dangerous than ever before because never before have we had weapons of total destruction. Most believe that nuclear war itself—not the Soviets or the Americans—is the enemy.

You can't qualify as a conscientious objector just because you object to nuclear war. But it's true that nuclear weapons have changed the nature of war and made it dangerous beyond its own destructiveness. A "conventional" war between the U.S. and the Soviet Union could quickly become a nuclear war. In a tense world, any war, even a small one, could become a confrontation and bring a nuclear holocaust closer.

So, if you are against nuclear war, you may find that you're also against all modern wars. And modern wars are the ones that matter most.

No Going Back

In war throughout history, there has never been any going back. Gunpowder might have been "limited" at first, but by World War I the only limits on its use were caused by lack of supplies. Tanks, the airplane, the submarine, even the railroad—all changed war for all time. So have nuclear weapons.

Nuclear strategists talk a lot about "limited" nuclear war, "tactical" nuclear weapons, and other ways in which a nuclear war would not be an all-out holocaust. But keeping nuclear weapons under control, once the shooting started, would be very difficult. Lord Mountbatten thought it might be impossible:

> I have never been able to accept the ... belief that ... nuclear weapons can be categorized in terms of their tactical or strategic purposes. ...
>
> I know how impossible it is to pursue military operations in accordance with fixed plans and agreements. In warfare the unexpected is the rule and no one can anticipate what an opponent's reaction will be to the unexpected.

No matter what the strategists may think now, Mountbatten says, if there were a war many things could not be predicted. And, though that might mean there would be no nuclear war at all, it might mean just the opposite. Is the risk worth taking? You will need to think about this question as you decide where you stand.

You and Nuclear War

When you're thinking about yourself and nuclear war, you need to ask yourself a number of questions. Do you think that deterrence will go on working? Or is it itself a danger? Do you think a large conventional war between the superpowers could be kept from becoming a nuclear war? Do you think that a nuclear war could be limited?

Many people answer these questions by saying that we ought to have all the nuclear weapons we can make, and be prepared to use them. Many others say that this is wrong—that the survival of humanity is more important than "victory" (whatever that means in a nuclear war) for one nation.

What do you think?

CHAPTER 11
FORCE, VIOLENCE, AND WAR

Many COs are puzzled by issues like whether it is right to use force in self-defense, whether a violent revolution can be justified, and whether there is any difference between police force and military force. Under the law, you don't even have to have answers to these questions to qualify as a CO. You can believe that self-defense is justified, for instance, or be against it, or not know what you would do.

But it's good to think about force and violence even though you don't have to. People often ask what you would do if you were personally attacked, and sometimes a local board will fire tricky questions at you—many of them questions on force and violence.

What Is Force?

One reason why force and violence are so hard to grapple with is that "force" has many meanings. Webster's Collegiate Dictionary gives eight separate meanings to the word "force." They range from the force used by a good public speaker to the force used in war. In physics, "force" is the power which causes a body to accelerate. Force can be applied against other nations, crowds, groups of people, or individuals. It can be violent or non-violent.

These many meanings of the word "force" make it important for you to decide for yourself which uses of force are right, and which are wrong. One thing you can't do is oppose all force. If you did, you couldn't even make a "forceful" speech, or use "forceful" arguments in discussions with your friends. One definition of force includes the force of a persuasive argument or speech.

Force and Violence

Many COs begin by distinguishing between violent and non-violent force. They oppose violent force and support non-violent force. This is a useful line to draw, but you need to be clear which uses of force you think are violent, and which you think are non-violent.

As you'll see below, for example, many people believe that injustice is a form of violence, even when no guns are used to enforce it. Others disagree. What's your opinion?

It isn't very useful to say simply that you're against all violence. What do you think is violent? How do you decide whether a particular use of force is violent? Your local board may try to trip you up on questions like these, so it's good to think about them ahead of time.

Even though this seems hard when it's written out on paper, you'll probably find that in practice it's easier to see where you stand. You need to think not only with your mind, but with your feelings. Often your heart will tell you what to do when your head is completely stymied.

Self-Defense

One question which nearly everyone asks a CO is,

"What would you do if your wife (or mother or granddaughter or daughter) was being raped?" For women the question would, of course, be different, but the idea would be the same.

It's a hard question to answer because it's really two questions: What do you think you ought to do?, and, What do you think you really would do? But these are hard questions for anyone—not just for COs. You may say you would respond non-violently, but in practice you might even kill the attacker. Someone who says he or she would probably use violence might decide in practice that non-violence is the best response.

That's true of all self-defense. You can know what you ought to do, but you can't know what you actually would do—with one exception. If you or one of your loved ones were attacked, you probably wouldn't napalm the attacker, or dig a trench around his house and bombard him with artillery fire, or torture and kill his family. And the courts agree. For the law, as well as common sense, defending yourself in a back alley is not the same as making war. A soldier needn't wait to be attacked when he is ordered to kill the enemy.

Revolutionary Violence

In a complex, changing world, violent revolution against injustice is one of the hardest issues you will face. Revolutionary violence now ranges from the traditional overthrow of the government (like the French and Russian revolutions) to hostage-taking or planting bombs in supermarkets. Even rioting like that in Miami in 1980 is a violent protest against injustice. What are you to make of all this? Is it right or wrong? Do you support or oppose revolutionary violence? And what kinds of violence do you mean?

How—if you support some forms of violence—are they different from war?

Many people find this issue very hard because they believe that an unjust society is itself a kind of violence. The French Socialist Proudhon once said, "Property is theft." He was not justifying theft, but he was saying that people who have a lot often have it at the expense of others who have little or nothing. You don't have to agree with Proudhon to see that he was pointing at an issue that troubles many people —COs and non-COs alike. If you say you're against injustice, somebody is sure to ask you how you feel about revolutionary violence.

It may help if you think about the difference between supporting violence and understanding its causes. Many people, including those who believe in non-violence, get the two confused. If someone is angry, his or her natural impulse is to strike out at whatever caused the anger—or at something else that is an easy target. So, for instance, blacks in Miami in 1980 lived in bad housing, had high unemployment, and felt they were victims of discrimination. When four police were acquitted of killing a black man during an arrest, many blacks in Miami rioted. They were outraged by the court decision, of course, but there were other causes for their anger.

To understand why people are angry, however, isn't the same as saying that their violent responses are right or even sensible. Many thinkers have argued that violent means always corrupt whatever end they are seeking. And history seems to bear this out. The French Revolution led to the Reign of Terror and Napoleon; the Russian Revolution led to Stalin. Many would say that the riots in Watts and other places during the 1960s have led to less change than the non-violent civil rights movement—or than one

Supreme Court decision in 1954. Do you agree or disagree?

Police Force

COs are often asked if they see any difference between the police and the military. You may not, and, particularly today, that's not surprising. Often the police are used to suppress efforts for justice. Most police forces are organized very much like the military. Some police forces give their members military-style training. Specialized police units like SWAT teams use military-style tactics. And, when all else fails, the police are prepared to shoot and kill a suspect.

But, on paper at least, it's not that simple. The police are enforcing laws, many of them designed to protect the whole community from wrongdoing. They work under legal controls very different from the "laws of war." Much of their work involves enforcing traffic laws, resolving disputes between people, and other basically non-violent actions.

If a police officer shoots someone illegally, he or she may be suspended from the force or even prosecuted. That isn't true of soldiers in war. An army doesn't distinguish between guilty and innocent enemies. If a soldier kills a civilian—which is still technically against the laws of war—he or she may or may not face legal action. To some extent it will depend on who wins the war. Even the most famous War Crimes trials, those at Nuremberg, would have been completely different if the Axis had won the Second World War. And many technical war crimes, like bombing of non-military targets, are now accepted military practice.

This isn't to say that you should (or shouldn't)

support police force. But as you think about police force and military force, keep in mind that, even though they may be very close in practice, they are different in principle. You can be against all police force, both in practice and in principle. Or you can support the principle of police force while opposing some of the ways it is applied. You can support all police force in practice and in principle. There are good reasons for all three positions. But don't confuse police force and military force and make a tricky question even trickier.

Military Force

One real difference between police force and military force is that the police are under community control (at least on paper) and the military, when it invades another country, is not under the control of the community where it is operating. This means that, for the military, the end—the "mission," or winning the war—is most important, and the means to the end is whatever force the commanders feel is needed.

A concrete example will make this more clear. In Vietnam, villages were often "pacified"—another way of saying that the population was uprooted and taken to an internment camp, where they were questioned (often using torture) and some were killed. This was shocking to the public, but to many who knew the history of war it wasn't surprising. The military wasn't a police force. It was operating under American, not Vietnamese, orders. Its orders were to defeat an enemy. "Pacification" was one means to that end.

That's also true with other military force which you may find shocking. Sherman's March to the Sea, which cut a wide swath of burned and devastated land from Atlanta to the Georgia Coast, is today considered not only good military strategy, but an important development in the "art of war." We are shocked by the use of poison gas, but in fact, in the only war when it was used on a large scale, gas was not a very effective weapon. Artillery and machine-gun fire killed far more people than gas in World War I. Gas is now against the "laws of war," while artillery and machine-gun fire are not. The "rights" and "wrongs" of military force aren't judged the way you would normally judge right and wrong. That's probably why you're reading this book in the first place.

Your Own Stand

No matter where you come out on the use of force, keep in mind that force—even violent force—and war are two different things. You can be puzzled about which use of force is right and which is wrong, while at the same time you may know that war is wrong. The important point for the law, and for your own thinking, is where you stand on war.

Don't let tricky questions on force and violence confuse the central issue.

CHAPTER 12
HITLER

One question which you're almost sure to face—from your local board, from your neighbors, and even from yourself—is whether you would have fought against Hitler.

In a way, it's an unfair question. Many people who fought in World War II now believe that all war is wrong. Others who refused to fight now think they made a mistake and should have fought. There's nothing you can do to change what happened in Europe in 1939 or 1940. It's all in the past, and war today is completely different from what it was then. How can you know what you would have thought? How can anyone expect you to know?

You can try to think what you would have done if you had held your current beliefs. But even that isn't easy. People at the time had very different reactions to Hitler, and they didn't know, in 1938 or 1939, what would happen in 1941 or 1945. We now see Hitler differently from the way people did at the time. So, though you can try to think how your beliefs would have applied then, you can't really be sure.

The courts disagree on whether you have to be sure. If you aren't, though, there's a good chance that you can still qualify as a CO. For details, see Chapter 6.

Hitler is a hard problem because, except for a few

129

modern Nazis, everyone now agrees that he did great evil. And most people think of World War II as the "good" war. It's even become a fad, as you can see in any bookstore.

Was it really that simple? What can we learn from the history of Europe in the 1930s and 1940s? This chapter can't answer these questions for you, but it can give you a start.

Hitler as Symbol and Reality

Many people today think of Adolf Hitler as the most evil man who ever lived. When the Defense Department plans a mobilization for war in Europe, it's planning how to stop a Hitler-style *Blitzkrieg* (lightning war). Visitors to Leningrad are always taken to see the monument to those who died in the Siege of Leningrad—caused, the guides remind visitors, by Hitler's armies. People in Israel today still recall Hitler's death camps. Even the name of Hitler—or his ministers like Goebbels, Himmler, and Goering—has come to mean pure evil.

This is an exaggeration, but not by much. Hitler was a ruthless man with dangerous ideas. He was at the center of a war which killed 38 million people. Millions of people died in German concentration camps—six million Jews, 200,000 Gypsies, and at least a million political prisoners. Hitler is not only a symbol of evil, but, in many ways, was the reality of it as well.

Hitler and World War II

World War II is often called "Hitler's War." Some historians believe that Hitler planned to conquer most of Europe, defeat the Soviet Union, and set up a

German Empire—without war if he could do it, but by making war if he could not. This is also what the public thinks: the cause of the war, and the reason it was fought, was Hitler.

But, like many things in history, the answer may not have been that easy. One school of historians thinks that, though Hitler meant to expand German power, he didn't plan the war that actually happened. Allied policy, they say, has to share the blame for World War II.

The truth is probably somewhere between these two extremes. But even if Hitler planned the war and started it by himself, a bigger question remains: Why did he come to power in the first place? And why did the German people follow his leadership? If any question is important for today, it's this.

The Coming of the War

Historians often say that World War I and World War II were really two parts of a single process. They believe the "German problem" began in the 19th Century, and it was still there even after the slaughter in the trenches of World War I. It led to World War II and Hitler. In its simplest form, the "problem" was this: Germany was becoming the most powerful country in Europe, but the other countries didn't want it to.

World War I was the largest European war up to its time. Ten million soldiers died in it. Great Britain and France actually lost more people in World War I than in World War II. The Treaty of Versailles, in 1919, tried to prevent another such war by disarming Germany, forcing her to pay war reparations, and setting up a new system, the League of Nations, to keep the peace in Europe. At the same time, the

Allies did not disarm, and the Treaty took territory from Germany. In Germany, and later on in the rest of Europe, most people thought the Treaty of Versailles was unfair.

During the 1920s, Germany had a domestic constitution much like that of the United States. She also had serious domestic problems. Her army had been disbanded, but thousands of ex-soldiers formed themselves into *Freikorps* (free corps), or private armies who began as border guards but later became, in many cases, right-wing political parties backed by force. German inflation in the 1920s became so bad that

> Men and women rushed to spend their wages, if possible within minutes of receiving them. Notes were trundled to the stores in wheelbarrows—or baby carriages. ... [T]here was resort to virtually every printing press that was capable of printing money. Notes were in literal fact churned out. And, on occasion, trade stopped as the presses fell behind in producing new bills.

The inflation ended in 1925, but in 1929 the Great Depression began. Not only America, but the rest of the Western world, suffered high unemployment and economic collapse. In Germany,

> by 1930 what had been a bothersome problem turned into an acute disaster. In just one month, January, the number of unemployed soared from 1.5 million to almost 2.5 million. From then on, the figures kept climbing steadily.

Germans blamed the unemployment on many things. Some thought war reparations caused it. Some blamed it on dishonest, incompetent politicians. Still others blamed the Jews. Many believed the Nazi propaganda.

Looking back, it's hard to imagine, but Hitler was a popular figure in the early 1930s. His party never got a majority in a free election, but by 1930 it had won 107 seats in the German parliament. He came to power when the President of Germany, Hindenburg, appointed him Chancellor. Once in power, he gradually built up his dictatorship and began his campaign against the Jews. But he also reduced unemployment by increasing public spending. He built public works like the *Autobahn* (a highway system) that are remembered today.

Overseas, he had many sympathizers—ranging from industrialists like Henry Ford to the writer Anne Morrow Lindbergh, wife of Charles Lindbergh. In an article in *Reader's Digest*, Lindbergh wrote:

> Much that is happening in Hitler's Germany is bad. ... but perhaps it will lead to some ultimate good. We, as Americans, do not have the moral right to judge what is happening. ...
> What was pushing behind Communism? What's behind fascism in Italy? What's behind nazism? ...
> Something one feels is pushing up through the crust of custom. ... One does not know what ... some new conception of humanity and its place on earth. I believe that it is, in its essence, good.

Lindbergh, who has devoted her life to humanitarian causes, later came to regret these words. But she wasn't alone. Many people deceived themselves about Hitler. Many others secretly agreed with him.

Appeasement

Today we think of "appeasement" as a kind of cowardice. Most people believe that the "appeasers" gave in to Hitler's demands, especially at Munich in 1938, and helped to bring on the war. Negotiations between countries today are much more difficult because neither side wants to be accused of "appeasement."

The truth isn't quite so simple. Hitler made many demands in the late 1930s, but the Munich agreement, which gave him parts of Czechoslovakia, was actually a British and French proposal. And it had much public support. "[F]ew causes have been more popular. Every newspaper [in Britain] applauded the Munich settlement with the exception of *Reynolds' News*." In the 19th and early 20th centuries, many great powers settled their differences by dividing up smaller powers or colonies. You may think this was very wrong, but it was common. In many ways, "appeasement" was like traditional diplomacy.

A Dilemma

It's easy to look back and criticize Neville Chamberlain, the British Prime Minister who proposed the Munich settlement. But at the time, Chamberlain was faced with a terrible dilemma. He couldn't have known what would happen in the future. He couldn't have known whether a "firm stand" would have stopped Hitler. We don't even know that today. What Chamberlain did know was that his country had been through the most bloody war in history in 1914-1918. The Munich settlement was his way of avoiding another great war. It didn't, of course, work out that way.

When a leader like Hitler is in power, armed with a mass army, there *isn't* any good solution to the problems he creates. World War II killed 38 million people. It's hard to think of this as good, even though most people do. So it wasn't a choice of a "good" war or a "bad" non-war. *Both* choices were bad because each might have led to great suffering.

It's possible that a different stand by the Allies at Munich would have prevented World War II. It's also possible that the war would have started sooner if the Allies had threatened Hitler with military force. No one will ever know. What we can learn today is that Hitler might not have been a problem if the Allies had followed different policies after World War I—for instance, if they'd followed through on their pledges about disarmament and the League of Nations. And we can see how the policies that they did follow laid the groundwork for the crisis of 1938 and the war that followed.

Can you be personally responsible for the results of policies that you disagree with and didn't make? What is your responsibility? These are questions for you to decide. But it's important to remember that Hitler didn't just happen. Allied policy, including that of the United States, must share some of the blame for Hitler's rise to power and the damage that he did.

It's interesting to know, also, that—even when their policies had failed—the Allies didn't at first see the war as a crusade. The war didn't, for instance, stop the Holocaust; and before the war, the Allies had done little or nothing to save the Jews of Europe. Britain declared war when Germany invaded Poland, but "as late as 1940, when France fell, some British political leaders gave thought and utterance to coming to terms with Hitler and letting him be." The United

States kept out of the war until the Japanese attack on Pearl Harbor in 1941. Even then, Hitler declared war on the U.S. before the U.S. declared war on Germany.

The Blitzkrieg

In 1939 and 1940, Hitler's armies seemed invincible. Their tactics often seemed cruel as well. *Blitzkrieg* has come to mean war which is not only rapid, using tanks to destroy opposition, but war which is especially ruthless. History, however, shows that the *Blitzkrieg* was no more cruel than any other tactic in war.

Hitler's method was designed to win battles with small numbers of troops. It made up for small forces by using a large number of tanks, moving rapidly, and seeking first to "penetrate the enemy's lines and destroy his communications." Hitler did not invent it. Three English military thinkers—Capt. B. H. Liddell Hart, Maj.-Gen. J. F. C. Fuller, and Maj.-Gen. G. leQ. Martel—and the French General Charles DeGaulle were the first to suggest this use of tanks. The Allies had first used a mass tank attack at the Battle of Cambrai in 1917.

The number of casualties caused by the *Blitzkrieg* was surprisingly low. In two months of fighting in Norway, for instance, the British lost 1,869; the Germans 5,296; and the other Allies, 2,030. By contrast, in *one day* of fighting at the Battle of the Somme in 1916, the British lost 60,000 killed and wounded. "[T]he blitzkrieg (sic) operations hurt the conquered less than had many wars of the past. What hurt them were the deprivations and the tyranny of the occupation that followed."

None of this means that the *Blitzkrieg* was a "kind" way of making war. There is no such thing. But

Hitler's early tactics were not original with him—in fact, most modern armies use something like them—and in many ways they were less terrible than the trench warfare of 1914-1918. The real destruction happened as the war dragged on.

The Horrors of War

Like most modern wars, World War II was a total war, as described in Chapter 9. It aimed not only at the enemy's armies, but at the people of the enemy's country. So it's not surprising that millions of civilians were killed.

Hitler's armies and his later policies were certainly more cruel than those of the Allies. One psychologist, Erich Fromm, points out that Hitler destroyed not only others but himself. He ordered the Holocaust. Toward the end of his career, he gave orders for all of Germany to be leveled rather than surrender. And he destroyed himself, not only by his own suicide, but by suicidal strategies like his attack on Moscow. At the same time, German soldiers became known for their ill-treatment of prisoners and civilians—following policies laid down by Hitler and Himmler.

Yet many of the policies of the Allies caused terrible damage—more, according to many historians, than was needed to win the war. The so-called "area bombing" campaign is an example. In 1940, the British set out to destroy German military targets—oil refineries, munitions plants, etc.—by bombing raids. They soon found that, if they flew by day, their bombers would be shot down. And if they flew by night, their bombers didn't have the equipment to bomb accurately. Rather than give up the bombing raids, Bomber Command changed its targets to German cities. This was supposed to break German morale and win the war.

In fact, "area bombing" probably did no such thing. "Did the bombers win the war? ... The answer ... is no. The German armies were fatally defeated by the Russians in July 1943 and at that point the bomber onslaught had barely begun and had caused no decisive damage." What the bombing did do was kill hundreds of thousands of civilians and destroy hundreds of German cities—many, like Dresden, of no military importance. The bombing campaign was controversial even during the war. Its critics ranged from pacifists to military thinkers like Liddell Hart.

This doesn't, of course, prove that the Nazis were really "good" and the Allies really "bad"—or even that, morally, there was nothing to choose between them. But it shows that, in modern war, nobody's hands are clean.

The Holocaust

Many people believe that the war against Germany stopped Hitler's campaign to exterminate the Jews of Europe. And that's true enough. After Germany had been defeated and Hitler had killed himself, the Allied troops liberated the extermination camps. Many of the soldiers wept uncontrollably at what they saw.

What these soldiers may not have known was that, before the war and during it, many of the Allied countries did little or nothing to help save the Jews or other threatened peoples like the Gypsies. Before the war,

> No country could be found willing to take substantial numbers of Jews; the British barred Palestine to them except in small numbers ... : the Americans ... require[d] certificates of birth which

few German Jews possessed and none could ask for from a German official ... ; a Bill to permit 20,000 Jewish children to enter the United States was killed by a "patriotic" lobby in the Congress on the grounds that it offended against the sanctity of family ties.

Before the war, no country did very much to help. And the war didn't stop the Holocaust until six million Jews and millions of other peoples had died in Nazi death camps.

In fact, after the war began, Hitler's campaign against "inferior" races grew more intense. The first concentration camp, at Dachau, had been set up in 1933 to hold not only Jews but Hitler's political opponents. The death camp at Auschwitz was set up in 1939, but it was not until later that the Nazis decided to go ahead with the "final solution." Historians have found no written order for the Holocaust, but "the decision ... [to] kill the Jews was probably reached after December 18, 1940 ... and before March 1, 1941."

On August 8, 1942, Gerhart Riegner of the World Jewish Congress reported on Hitler's extermination plans to the United States government. At first American officials didn't believe the report. But even after it was confirmed, they didn't try to organize a rescue effort. One critic says,

> As [Hitler] moved ... toward the total destruction of the Jews, the government and the people of the United States remained bystanders. Oblivious to the evidence which poured from official and unofficial sources, Americans went about their business unmoved and unconcerned.

As the war went on, the death camps worked faster and faster.

What can we make of the Holocaust today? The war didn't prevent it. The war also didn't start it. If there had been no war, the Nazis might have killed millions of "inferior races" anyway. And Hitler's Holocaust —though it was the most terrible—was not the first. In the middle ages, Jews were often slaughtered and driven from their homes. Between 1915 and 1918, the Turkish government massacred two million Armenians. And there have been other examples throughout history.

Nor was Hitler the last to try to kill a whole people. Today we have seen extermination campaigns in Uganda, Burundi, Cambodia, and Brazil—and there may be others which haven't been widely reported.

At least one lesson of the Holocaust is that racial hatred is always dangerous. Anti-semitism had been common in Germany and most of Europe for centuries before Hitler. Hitler wasn't that much different in his thinking from the anti-semitic composer Johannes Brahms. But he acted on his convictions, and others followed his lead.

Another Hitler Today?

When you're thinking about Hitler, you'll probably ask yourself whether another Hitler is possible today. After all, even if you wanted to fight the historical Hitler, you couldn't. He's been dead for thirty-five years, and the "German problem" has been replaced by the Cold War.

Part of the Cold War is the threat of nuclear war. And that makes today completely different from 1939. Many people in the U.S. think of the Soviet Union's leadership as today's Hitler. And many Soviet citizens think of the U.S. leadership as today's Hitler. But the leaders of the superpowers don't play the kinds of bluffing games that led to war in 1939. They fear each other, but they aren't madmen. If it's sane to build weapons that could destroy civilization, then they're sane by today's standards.

Hitler wasn't completely sane. If he had had nuclear weapons, he would probably have used them. In 1939, he could threaten the whole of Europe without nuclear weapons. Today, a Hitler without nuclear weapons would be terrible in his own country but would pose little threat to the world. A Hitler with the U.S. or Soviet arsenal would be a threat such as the world has never known before.

How would you—or anyone, for that matter—stop him? The other countries of the world would probably threaten him with nuclear weapons. If war came, it would be nuclear, and it wouldn't matter very much whether you or anyone else decided to fight. Hundreds of millions would be dead before the armies could march. This would "stop" a new Hitler. It would also "stop" much of the human race.

Many people think that a new Hitler is less of a danger to the world than "sane" world leaders with their fingers on the nuclear button. What do you think?

We can learn a lot from history. But, in a world of nuclear weapons, shortages, and interdependent nations, history can't tell us much about the future. And it's the future you need to be concerned about.

CHAPTER 13
IF THE COUNTRY WERE ATTACKED

The question of Hitler is probably the hardest one when you're thinking about conscientious objection. Almost as difficult is the question, "Would you fight if the country were attacked?"

It's a hard question for three reasons. You can't know what your beliefs will be in the future. When a local board or your next-door neighbor asks the question, they usually don't say what kind of attack they mean. And hidden in the question is another: Don't you love your country enough to help it when it's threatened?

To be a conscientious objector, you don't have to know what you would do in the future. But you may want to think about your position. There's no way to do this that will work for everyone. Some people try to think of wars that might happen and ask themselves what they would do. This chapter tries to see what is really likely. For the law on hypothetical questions, read Chapter 6.

Real and Imaginary Attacks

The last time the United States was attacked was 1941, when the Japanese bombed Pearl Harbor. Although some historians now believe that U.S. officials knew Pearl Harbor might be attacked, and could have prevented the attack, Congress and the public didn't know this at the time. They supported a declaration of war against Japan.

In the nuclear age, however, an attack like Pearl Harbor is pretty unlikely. The attacking enemy would probably use nuclear bombs and missiles, and the war that resulted could be over in half an hour. Military planners on both sides think in terms of nuclear weapons when they think about making a direct attack—or responding to an attack—on the other side's territory. So another Pearl Harbor—an attack on the U.S. which led to a long conventional war—is very unlikely.

You could even say it is impossible in the nuclear age. If the U.S. were attacked with nuclear missiles, it would respond with nuclear missiles. If it were invaded by a conventional army, it would still probably launch nuclear missiles against the invader's home territory.

But even supposing that both sides agreed not to use nuclear weapons, how likely is a direct attack on U.S. territory?

An attack over land seems pretty unlikely. Our only land neighbors are Canada and Mexico. The U.S. has had unarmed borders with both for over a hundred years.

But what, your local board might ask, about the Russians? Most Americans are afraid of the Soviet Union, but a Soviet invasion of the U.S. would be a military disaster. Even the Bering Straits in Alaska provide a tough barrier against attacks either way. Cuba, which might provide a base for an attack, is 90 miles from the Florida coast. And getting a large military force to Cuba from the Soviet Union wouldn't be easy.

If the Country Were Attacked—145

With or without a base in Cuba, a "conventional" Soviet invasion of the U.S. would face problems greater than any military operation in history. If the invasion force traveled by ship, the weather, the chance that the beaches would be defended, and the long distance to be covered would probably stop it before it started. If the attackers traveled by air, the cost in fuel would be enormous. Thousands of airplanes would be needed to carry hundreds of thousands of soldiers, their supplies, thousands of tanks and guns, and millions of tons of ammunition. And what would the soldiers eat when they arrived? How would they keep from running out of ammunition? To solve these problems, hundreds or even thousands of planes would need to fly the Atlantic *every day*.

All this would be true even if the United States resisted the invasion nonviolently—for instance, by hiding or destroying food supplies. A military operation, no matter how it's resisted, needs a good supply line. Hundreds of military campaigns have broken down because the soldiers had no ammunition and no food. The most famous is probably Napoleon's invasion of Russia in 1812.

Military historians now consider Napoleon's march to Moscow one of the most foolish plans in history. Yet the problems facing Napoleon were simple compared with those that would face an army attacking the U.S. over water. No general would plan such an operation. If one proposed it seriously, he would probably be removed from his post and sent on a long vacation.

Provoked and Unprovoked

Your local board and your neighbor, when they ask

you about an attack on the country, are probably thinking of an unprovoked attack. But politics and military affairs are more complex than that. Suppose that, in 1970, the North Vietnamese government had bombed San Francisco and mined San Francisco Bay. Would this have been an unprovoked attack? You'd probably say it wasn't because the U.S. had been bombing Hanoi and mining North Vietnamese harbors since the late 1960s. Would you fight if there were such an attack?

It's hard to imagine a future attack on this country that wouldn't be provoked in some way by its policies. We like to think of the U.S. as a peaceful country, but in fact, since World War II, this country has used or threatened military force over 200 times. In some cases, like Korea and Vietnam, U.S. troops have gone to foreign countries and fought. In others, the U.S. has sent an aircraft carrier or moved a battalion of Marines. And in the Cuban missile crisis of 1962, the U.S. actually threatened a nuclear attack on the Soviet Union.

What Could You Do?

Local boards often like to talk about scenes of rape, pillage, and destruction and ask COs what they would do. But war always involves destruction. A nuclear war, which would be the most destructive of all, would also be a war in which your willingness to fight would matter least. It would be over quickly, and the military probably wouldn't even have time to mobilize.

Unlikely as it is, a conventional attack on the U.S. would bring the horrors of war to this country's territory for the first time since the Civil War. The military would have time to mobilize. And you might change your mind about fighting, as people have done in the past. But if you still felt you couldn't fight, you could do much to relieve the suffering which the war would cause. You could tend the wounded, try to find shelter for people whose homes had been destroyed, and many other actions—all without being part of the military. And you could, if you wished, help organize non-violent resistance to the invaders.

"Vital Interests"

Another kind of "attack" on the U.S.—and a much more likely one—is an attack on the country's "vital interests." In 19th-Century Europe, "vital interests" meant colonial interests. Or a country might feel its "interests" were being attacked when another country tried to change the balance of power. More and more lately, however, the "vital interests" of the U.S. have come to mean natural resources like oil that are supplied by other countries.

But is war for oil possible? Many experts think it is not. Getting U.S. troops to the oil fields would be difficult, and guarding the oil against sabotage after a successful invasion would be nearly impossible.

U.S. military planners told the press in early 1980 that a war for the oil fields would include use of "tactical" nuclear weapons. As you've seen from Chapter 10, "tactical" nuclear weapons are in many cases bigger than the Hiroshima bomb. After a war in which the two sides fought with "tactical" nuclear weapons, there might not be any oil fields left. And what was left might be too radioactive to be of any use.

Is an attack on the oil fields really an attack on the U.S.? Is such an attack likely? And would war be a sensible response to it? What about alternatives

—like using less oil? The Center for Defense Information, a well-known research group, has said that the Pentagon's best contribution to keeping U.S. oil supplies safe would be for the military to use less oil. In 1976, the U.S. military used more oil than the entire country of Sweden.

Three Positions on War

Most people take one of three stands on war. The first position is that every U.S. war is a defensive war. Probably your local board believes this. Even the government wants people to believe it. The Pentagon, after all, is called the Department of Defense.

Chances are, if you're reading this book, that you disagree.

The second position, which most people take, is that some wars are defensive and justified, and others are not. But what, in the modern world, is a defensive war? If Iran attacked the United States with military force, would that be an unprovoked attack? Or would it be the result of U.S. support of the Shah? It's hard to judge.

And how likely is an unprovoked attack on the country? As you've seen, it's not likely at all. But if an unprovoked attack is very unlikely, then, in practice, people who would fight only a defensive war are pretty close to people who take the third position: rejection of all wars. In fact, the two groups are the same on one point: neither group really knows what its views would be in a future war.

In the 1930s, hundreds of thousands of men in England signed pledges never to fight again. When war came in 1939, some of these men refused to fight, but most joined the military. Were they insincere when they pledged never to fight? Probably not. But their views changed. And they couldn't have known this would happen.

And, though you know how you feel now, you can't really predict how you will feel ten years from now. That's true whether you now reject all wars or think you should support all U.S. wars. Before the Vietnam War, many Americans supported all U.S. wars. Most still do, but large numbers of people changed their minds because of the Indochina War.

How can you know what you would think in a future war? You can't. But to be a CO, you don't have to. You need to think about how you feel now—not in an imaginary future.

Are You Patriotic?

Your local board and your neighbor may not even have thought about what kind of attack they mean when they ask if you would defend the country. In their minds, whether or not you would fight in the military is the test of whether or not you support your country.

But it's not that simple. Very few COs are unpatriotic. Those who follow the law often feel they owe service to their country. Those who break the law often are protesting against a law they feel is undemocratic. And everyone who protests against war is protesting against U.S. policy—usually to change it for the better. If the only test of patriotism is willingness to serve in the military, then you're unpatriotic if you refuse. But that's not the only test. Or even a very good test.

In the nuclear age, as Chapter 10 pointed out, more and more weapons don't make the country more and more safe. If anything, they make it less safe because they would make war, if it comes, even more destructive.

Who, then, is patriotic? The person who believes in arms or the person who says No to the war system? Both may be and probably are. You must make your own decision based on your values—not on someone else's opinion of your patriotism.

Are You Afraid?

Many people think that COs aren't against war at all—that they're just afraid of dying. That's often what your neighbor means by asking if you would defend the country against an attack. It's a hard question because you don't always know why you do what you do.

But the fact is that *everyone* is afraid of death and of being wounded. That's why soldiers are drilled and grouped into platoons and brigades—so that, by following orders and being part of the group, they can forget that they're afraid. It's not natural to move toward a machine gun that is firing at you, but soldiers are sometimes ordered to do it. And many of them would run away if their actions weren't almost automatic. Or if they were alone.

Most soldiers today, in any case, don't see combat at all. They're support troops—clerks, mechanics, etc. And when there's no war going on, the greatest chance of death in the military is from an accident.

If you're disturbed by the question of cowardice, don't let it worry you. You're not alone. The real question for you is not how you feel about dying, but how you feel about killing.

PART IV

COs IN COURT AND PRISON

CHAPTER 14
COs AND THE COURTS

If you had been drafted during the First World War, your induction order would have put you automatically in the military. In 1917-1918, 446 conscientious objectors were court-martialed and sent to military prison. 4,750 civilians, many of them non-registrants, were convicted by civilian courts and received fines or prison sentences.

During World War II, as at present, men ordered to report for induction did not become subject to military law until they actually accepted induction. U.S. courts sent 6,000 COs to prison, about two-thirds of them Jehovah's Witnesses.

Objectors have been sent to prison under all modern draft laws. The largest single group of them is Jehovah's Witnesses. The second largest is made up of draft resisters who refused to register; and the smallest group is made up of COs who applied to their draft boards for CO status but were denied. This has happened mainly because the courts now pay careful attention to whether or not an induction order was legally issued.

Toward the end of the Vietnam era, the number of draft violators in prison had dropped, even though the number of people who refused the draft had increased. More resisters were acquitted, and more of those who were convicted were sentenced to probation.

Even if no one is being drafted now, you probably want to know what might happen to you if the draft began again and you felt you had to resist it—either by refusing to register, or by refusing an induction order. This chapter explains federal court procedures and the kinds of defenses which COs have used in court. It is no substitute for a good lawyer. If you feel that you must break the law, CCCO can help you find an attorney.

Not all federal courts have the same procedures. For information on local conditions, you'll need to see a local counselor or lawyer.

Judicial Review

The Military Selective Service Act says that decisions of local and appeal boards are "final." This doesn't mean, however, that your draft board can simply do what it wants. A series of Supreme Court decisions in the late 1940s allows the courts to look at your local board's decision and reverse it if there is "no basis in fact" for the local board's action.

The actual wording of the law [section 10(b)(3)] is as follows: "No judicial review shall be made of the classification or processing of any registrant ... except as a defense to a criminal prosecution ... *Provided*, That such review shall [consider things normally decided by draft boards only] when there is no basis in fact for the classification assigned."

This provision, placed in the law in 1967, finally brought the draft law into line with the 1946 Supreme Court decision in *Estep v. U.S.* A still earlier decision, *Falbo v. U.S.* (1944), established the requirement that you must "exhaust administrative remedies" in order to defend yourself in court. This means that you must follow the appeal procedures and, in some districts, cooperate with the Army's induction examination up to the point where you are asked to step forward for induction.

Getting a Case to Court

It sounds like there's only one way to get your case to court if you think your induction order is illegal: refuse induction. But that's not always true. In some cases, the courts have even blocked induction orders which had already been issued. These are exceptions to the rule, though. Unless your local board acted "lawlessly," you'll probably have to decide whether to accept or refuse induction once you've been denied CO status.

There are usually two ways of getting your case to court. The first is to refuse induction and defend yourself against criminal charges. The second is to accept induction, go into the military, and have your lawyer ask federal court for a writ of habeas corpus. The arguments in support of habeas corpus would be the same as those you would use for a criminal defense. If you win a habeas corpus action, you would be released from the military because you were being held there illegally. And even though you're a CO, the courts will not hold it against you if you decide to accept induction and petition for release afterwards.

This doesn't mean that there's nothing to choose between the two alternatives. But the choice is yours, based on how you feel — not on how it will affect your legal case. You'll need to think mostly about where you'd want to be if you lost your case. If you're against military duty and would rather be in jail than accept it, you should probably refuse induction. If you're willing to accept military duty if you lose, you probably should choose habeas corpus action. The choice is that clear, but, of course, it's not easy.

Luckily, you don't have to make it when you're first deciding whether or not you're a CO. You can decide that you're against war and leave other questions for later if you want to. As you go through the CO processing, or even as you think more about what you believe, your choice will probably become clearer to you. Meantime, you will strengthen your case if you follow all appeal channels. When you're coming to the end of your appeals within the draft system, you'll need to talk to your counselor or your lawyer about your options and to make your decision—if you haven't already made it.

Reading the next chapter of this *Handbook* may help in your decision. It will at least give you an idea what you may be getting into.

Criminal Prosecution

For simplicity, let's assume you've decided to refuse induction. What happens next?

You could be prosecuted for any violation of the draft law which you've committed—for instance, failing to report a change of address. Normally, though, if you refuse to report a change of address or commit another "minor" violation of the law, you'll be processed like anyone else and, if your lottery number is reached, ordered to report for induction. The government doesn't often prosecute "minor" draft violations, though they sometimes do. And sometimes you can be charged not only with refusing induction, but with another offense like failing to report a change of address.

If you refuse induction, Selective Service will review

your file to see that there were no errors in processing your case. Then your local board will send your file to the U.S. Attorney for prosecution. Your case will then become the responsibility of the Justice Department. If you're a non-registrant, the U.S. Attorney can and sometimes will start prosecution without recommendation from Selective Service. But this doesn't happen very often.

The U.S. Attorney is under the Attorney General in Washington, but the decision on your case will usually be a local decision. If the U.S. Attorney decides not to prosecute you, either for policy reasons or because you have a good defense, your file goes back to Selective Service for reprocessing. You, your counselor, or your attorney can try to persuade the U.S. Attorney not to prosecute if that seems appropriate.

Jurisdiction

A draft law violation is a felony. It is tried in a U.S. District Court. The district where you will be tried depends on where you broke the law. Usually this will be the court district where your local board is located, but there are some exceptions. If you refuse to register, you will be tried in the district where you were required to register. Since each case is different, it's best to consult your lawyer, your counselor, or CCCO about where your case will be tried.

If you are arrested in one district but face charges in another, you have the right to a hearing, mostly to determine if you're the person named in your indictment. You can waive this formality if you like.

You can ask that your case be transferred to the district where you were arrested. This procedure, called a change of venue, is only available if you agree to plead guilty or *nolo contendere*. The U.S. Attorneys for both districts must agree to it. If you intend to plead guilty and know that you'll get a lighter sentence where you were arrested, you might consider asking for a change of venue.

Consulting a Lawyer

It's usually a good idea to make arrangements ahead of time with your lawyer. If you're planning to seek habeas corpus, you should retain a lawyer at least two weeks before your induction date. If you plan to refuse induction, you should get a lawyer well before you're actually charged. This can take some weeks or even months, but it's good to have a lawyer even before you refuse induction.

You don't have to have a lawyer if you don't want one. But if you plan to challenge your induction order or the constitutionality of the draft law, or if you just don't feel you can speak for yourself in court, you should have legal counsel. Having a lawyer will improve your chances of a shorter prison sentence or probation instead of prison.

If you intend primarily to present your own religious, moral, or political reasons for breaking the draft law, you can defend yourself in court. Keep in mind, though, that you probably won't be acquitted. And you'll be under a lot of pressure from the judge —and maybe your family—to get a lawyer. If you're planning to defend yourself, you should go to at least one trial and see what happens. And you should talk to your counselor or CCCO about what may happen in court.

CCCO will help you find a lawyer if you want one. You will have to make your own arrangement with your lawyer, and you should agree with your attorney ahead of time on the fees for handling the case. Costs will often run to $1,000.00 or more. If you can't pay a fee this large, you may be able to find a lawyer who'll take your case for a nominal fee, or let you pay in monthly installmments over a long period of time. The court will appoint a lawyer if you can't afford your own counsel, and CCCO will help such a lawyer in any way possible.

FBI Investigation

An FBI investigation usually comes before indictment. You may be visited and asked to give a signed statement on your background, the circumstances of your refusal, and the reason you refused. You don't have to sign or give such a statement. You don't even have to answer any questions which the FBI asks you. In fact, most lawyers advise against telling them more than your name and address. The FBI doesn't decide what to do with your case, so don't rely on any promises they may make.

Preliminary Hearing and Indictment

The government can bring you to trial in three ways: a grand jury can hand down an indictment against you; they can file a complaint against you and hold a preliminary hearing, followed by a grand jury indictment or the filing of a "criminal information;" or the U.S. Attorney can file an information against you in the district court if you waive indictment. Most prosecutions follow the first of these procedures, but you could be arrested on a complaint and later indicted, as in the second.

The grand jury proceeding is usually a rubber

stamp. An indictment is an official charge that you have committed a crime. It will state what you are alleged to have done. The grand jury usually hears the evidence in a closed session, which neither you nor your lawyer can go to, and returns a "true bill" of indictment. Then the district court issues a warrant for your arrest.

If you haven't been indicted before your arrest, you may have a preliminary hearing before a U.S. Magistrate or judge. The government will present the evidence against you, and the judge will decide whether it is enough to hold you for grand jury action. Although you can't present your side of the story at this hearing, your lawyer can cross-examine government witnesses. Many COs waive this hearing, which is usually a meaningless ritual.

You may waive indictment even if you have already waived the preliminary hearing and may proceed by way of a "criminal information." But most prosecutions use the grand jury and indictment process.

Arrest

You can be arrested at any time following your violation of the draft law—sometimes months or even years afterward. In a few districts, draftees who refused induction were arrested on the spot during the Vietnam era. But usually there will be some time before your refusal and your arrest.

Arrest can occur at any time and place. It is usually made by two FBI agents. If you wish, your lawyer can arrange with the U.S. Attorney for you to surrender yourself rather than being arrested. Some COs think this is a form of collaboration and simply wait to be arrested.

Following your arrest, you'll usually be taken to a lockup at a federal court or local or county jail. You must be allowed one telephone call to your attorney or other "Bondsmen" (friends who will arrange bail). You must be told the charges against you, though you usually won't see the indictment until your bail hearing. Your friends can find out where you are by contacting the U.S. Marshal for the district where you are arrested. The Marshal's office is usually in the same building as the court.

You will be fingerprinted or photographed, sometimes more than once. FBI agents may interview you even if they have done so before. You don't have to answer any of their questions. It's best just to decline —politely—to talk with them.

Release on Bond

You must be brought before a court promptly for a bond hearing. A U.S. Magistrate usually conducts bond hearings. The Magistrate's Court is usually in the same building as the U.S. District Court and the U.S. Marshall's office. The grand jury could set your bail, but this happens very rarely.

At your bond hearing, you, your lawyer, and your friends may ask the Magistrate to release you on your own recognizance (promise to appear in court, without requiring cash bail). In some areas this is routine, but in others you may have to find bail money. If your bail seems unreasonable (over $1,000.00, or over $10,000.00 if a 10% deposit will be accepted), you and your lawyer should try to get it reduced. If the Magistrate refuses, you and your lawyer can ask a judge of the district court to reduce your bail.

Some COs refuse on principle to put up bail or sign a bond because they feel the bail system discriminates against the poor or because they will not use procedures set up by a court system they think is unjust. Most accept bail, however, or will at least sign a recognizance bond, so that they can arrange their defense and settle their affairs before trial. If you refuse bond, you may be jailed for weeks, or more usually months, waiting for your case to be tried. Time which you serve before your trial doesn't count as part of whatever sentence the judge imposes after your trial.

If the Magistrate or judge requires bail, you can provide it in three ways:

•*Cash Bail*, which should be either actual cash or a certified check for the exact amount of the bail. You should ask the Magistrate to whom the check should be made payable before you draw it. Churches, peace groups, friends, and relatives may help to raise the needed money. It's better not to post your personal funds because in some cases the judge might fine you (as part of your sentence) and the fine might be withheld from your bail money. If you can't be released on recognizance, cash bail is usually the best arrangement.

•*Property Bail*, which can be put up if the real estate is located in the federal district where you are being held. The assessed value of the property, less mortgages and in some states less homestead valuations, is used to determine the value of the property. It must be as great as or greater than the amount of the bail. Several properties may be used together to cover the bail. They need not be owned by the same owner. The owner of the property should appear before the Magistrate to sign the bond and bring the deed and tax receipts showing the assessed valuation. In some states, property owned by a married woman cannot be used, and some states make other property exempt from use for bail. Check local exemption laws if you are planning to use property bail.

•*Bail Bond,* which is a promise by a professional bondsman to pay the bail. Usually a bail bond costs a fee of 10% of the amount of the bond.

Whether or not you're required to put up bail, a bond may include troublesome conditions. For instance, you may be forbidden to leave the district without the judge's permission. After your case has been disposed of, your bond will be canceled and the entire cash bail, if any, returned. If you fail to appear in court or violate a condition of your bond, your bond may be canceled and your bail forfeited. "Bond jumping" is also a crime, punishable by fine and up to five years in prison.

The Arraignment

Your arraignment is usually the first time you will appear in district court. If bond has not been set before, it will be at the arraignment, but the purpose of most arraignments is to see if you have an attorney and how you intend to plead.

On the day of your arraignment, you will come to the courtroom and wait until your case is called by the clerk. You then come forward before the judge. If you have no lawyer and can't afford one, the judge must appoint a lawyer for you, at no expense to you, if you wish. You can waive your right to counsel and defend yourself, though the judge may pressure you to have a lawyer. Usually you can get a delay of at least one week if you're not ready to plead. You may even be able to get the U.S. Attorney to agree in advance to a delay.

While you are waiting for your arraignment, you

should go to several criminal trials to see first-hand what will happen to you. If you're waiting in jail for your trial, you may wish to arrange for a shave, clean shirt, etc., for your appearance in court.

Entering a Plea

At one point during your arraignment, the clerk of the court will ask you, "How do you plead, guilty or not guilty?" For many COs, this isn't as simple as it sounds. Your indictment charges you with a specific offense, such as refusing induction. You'll probably be willing to admit that you went to the induction center and refused to step forward when ordered. But you'll probably also think that your induction order was illegal, and if the court agrees you may be found not guilty. You may also think that even though you refused to do as you were told, you're not really guilty because what you did was morally right.

If you tried to obtain CO status, were turned down, and had to refuse induction, CCCO recommends that you plead not guilty in most cases. That's the only way that you can make any defense to the charges against you.

If you're charged with some other offense where you don't have a strong defense—for instance, failing to report a change of address—you may decide that you want to get your case over with. You could still plead not guilty if you felt strongly that you should present a defense. But if you want to put your case behind you quickly, you don't necessarily have to plead guilty to do it.

There are four possible courses of action:

•To plead Not Guilty: If you want to have a trial or take your case to a higher court, you must plead Not Guilty. A trial date will then be set, and you will be released on bond.

• To stand Mute: That is, to refuse to plead at all. In this case, the judge will order the clerk to enter a plea of Not Guilty, and a trial date will be set.

• To plead Guilty: In this case, there won't be a trial, and the only remaining matters are your statement to the court, a pre-sentence investigation, and sentencing. You could be sentenced immediately and begin serving your time; you could be sentenced immediately but given a few days to settle your affairs; or sentencing may be delayed for the pre-sentence investigation and you could be released on bond.

• To plead *Nolo Contendere,* or "I do not contest the charge": If this plea is accepted by the court, it has the same effect as a guilty plea. You may prefer it, however, because it doesn't say that you're guilty, yet admits the obvious fact that you didn't follow the law. If the judge refuses this plea, you will have to decide whether to plead Guilty or Not Guilty. If you refuse to decide, the judge will order a Not Guilty plea entered for you.

Trial

The procedures at arraignment and sentencing are simple. A trial on a Not Guilty plea is too complicated to summarize in this *Handbook*. You will need a lawyer if you plan to present legal arguments. The "motions" your lawyer makes, orally or in writing, are the heart of the case. Each one is a statement that the indictment should be dismissed or that you should be acquitted because Selective Service hasn't followed the law; because a certain regulation conflicts with the draft Act; or because some provision of the draft law is unconstitutional. Most motions are supported by "briefs," or summaries of the arguments and earlier cases which apply to your case.

A trial may be a "bench trial," in which the judge decides all the issues, or a jury trial, in which twelve citizens must agree on a verdict. The judge usually decides all motions and legal issues. The jury usually decides only whether you did what the indictment says you did. In rare cases, juries have decided to acquit defendants despite the facts, and they can do this if they feel the indictment was illegal or unjust. But you can't count on a jury doing this. Since most of the issues in your case will probably be legal issues, you'll probably want to waive your right to a jury trial and concentrate on persuading the judge that Selective Service acted illegally in your case. Some draft resisters, however, want a jury trial so they can try to reach the consciences of twelve people and gain an acquittal or mistrial when the jurors disagree.

At trial the government presents its case. This usually is made up of your draft file and a Selective Service employee (usually the local board clerk) called the "custodian" of your file—and little else. Someone who actually saw you refuse may also testify. You can cross-examine the government's witnesses and challenge the legality or accuracy of your file, and you can present your own witnesses. In most cases, though, the arguments will all be based on the record in the file, and witnesses won't be needed. A trial can last an hour or several days, depending on how many arguments each side presents.

The judge may hand down a verdict at the end of all the arguments, or may announce it days, weeks, or even months later. You probably won't be sentenced at the time of the verdict.

Defenses

There are three basic defenses in a draft case. The first is that there was "no basis in fact" for your classification or some other local board action in your case. The second is that Selective Service made an error in your processing which deprived you of your rights. Finally, you can be found not guilty if the local board or appeal board relied on a misinterpretation of the law in deciding your case.

The "basis in fact" defense goes back to the *Estep* case. In 1953, in *Dickinson v. U.S.*, the Supreme Court held that "the courts may properly insist that there be some proof that is incompatible with the registrant's proof of exemption." In other words, your local board's reason for denying your claim has to be backed up by evidence.

Selective Service can't deny your claim merely because they don't believe you. They have to state why they don't believe you, and what evidence there is against you. "It is well-settled that even under the 'no basis in fact' test, doubt as to sincerity cannot be predicated [based] on mere speculation." "The mere assertion of disbelief in the claimant's sincerity, no matter how persistently ... repeated, is not enough to overcome his ... case."

If you can show that Selective Service harmed your interests by making procedural errors in your case, you have a good chance for acquittal. Your local board must make its decisions in accord with the regulations and the draft law.

Among cases which have been won in court are those in which new information submitted by a registrant was not considered by his local board; the registrant was not told about or given a chance to reply to evidence against him; the local board clerk gave wrong information to the registrant; the local board didn't give reasons for denying a claim; the local board placed an illegal time limit on a personal appearance; the local board reopened the registrant's classification with no reason; the local board illegally refused to reopen classification.

Pre-Sentence Investigation

If you are convicted after trial, you may be sentenced and jailed immediately. Usually, however, you'll be allowed to remain free on bond until a later appearance for sentencing. Meanwhile, the judge will usually order a pre-sentence investigation by a U.S. Probation Officer.

Probation Officers supervise people on parole and on probation. They're usually the most liberal court officials you'll meet. The main part of the investigation is usually an interview, and if you cooperate with the interview you'll have a better chance of a light sentence or probation. Your friends and relatives can visit or write to the probation officer to urge leniency. They can also try to persuade the U.S. Attorney to recommend probation or a short sentence, or at least not to oppose it.

Sentencing

When you appear for sentencing, you can present statements in "mitigation" in which you explain why you should be put on probation. You can present witnesses or friends to speak on your behalf, explain the motives which led to your refusal, and present evidence that you are of good character.

The U.S. Attorney will also make a statement and may make a recommendation about your sentence.

This statement usually carries a great deal of weight.

It's important to know the difference between parole and probation. Parole is a "qualified" release from prison after you have served part of your term. If you are not sent to prison at all, but released under certain conditions, you are being placed on probation.

During the later years of the Vietnam era, about half of all draft violators were sentenced to probation, usually conditioned on two years of alternative-service-type work. There's no way to know what sentencing might be like in the future.

Appeal

If you are convicted of a draft violation, you have the right to appeal your conviction to a U.S. Circuit Court of Appeals. Many convictions have been reversed, especially where Selective Service didn't follow its own procedures or made an error of law. Appeals are expensive, and you may not want to appeal unless you have a good chance of winning. Consult your lawyer about your chances on appeal.

If your appeal fails, you can petition the Supreme Court for a "writ of certiorari." If the writ is granted, the Court will hear your case. The Supreme Court, unlike lower courts, decides which cases it will and won't hear, and unless your case raises important issues, it will probably deny the writ.

Repeated Prosecutions

If you win your case, your local board may finally give you the classification you want. It's possible, though, that they won't. Then you might be processed again and prosecuted for a second refusal. This might also happen if you've decided not to cooperate with the draft at all. The courts are very careful with repeat prosecutions where a registrant has been acquitted once, so new charges against you are not very likely. If you've served time in prison, the Justice Department's policy is not to charge you a second time.

Deciding What To Do

You don't have to decide now whether you'll refuse induction. But it's sometimes helpful for you to think about whether you'd be willing to face the worst that the government can do to you: a long prison sentence. If you're not sure, that's not surprising; and it's no reason to put off filing for CO status. A prison sentence is frightening, but if you're worried about it, that doesn't mean you're insincere.

But it is important to know what you may be in for if you find that you have to break the draft law. By reading this chapter and the next, you'll be prepared to make a good decision when you do have to decide.

CHAPTER 15
COs IN PRISON

If you refuse induction, refuse to register, or break the draft law in some other way, you may find yourself facing a term in prison. This chapter will give you an introduction to life in federal prisons, but no chapter in a book can tell you what prison life is really like. You can learn more by talking with other COs who have been in prison.

Many war resisters have served a term in prison, and most of these resisters were glad they went to prison rather than going into the military. You'll be better able to face prison life if you know what you're getting into and if you talk with people who have gone through the experience themselves. You can also contact Prisoner Visitation and Support, which visits federal prisoners across the U.S. For more on PVS, see the sections at the end of this chapter.

The Prison World

The details of life in prison vary from one to another, but all prisons have one thing in common: your life, and your time, will not be under your control. Prisoners have a lot of time to kill, but it is not "free time" as you usually think of it. There's no such thing in prison. You're always confined. If the guards are unfair in their treatment, you can't fight the injustice as you would on the outside—though there may be things you can do. You can only have visitors at certain times. And most of all, when you want to leave, you can't.

All this makes prison life hard. But chances are you won't be alone. Most prisoners share a common dislike for those who cage them, and war resisters are no exception. You'll do best if you have support on the outside, from your friends, from your counselor, from your family, and from your lawyer.

Prison officials often see war resisters as square pegs in round holes. Many war resisters find that they object to the prison system, and often COs have helped to organize resistance to injustices within the prison. Many war resisters make a "satisfactory institutional adjustment," but others don't. And prison officials regard COs as more intelligent and energetic than other prisoners. You'll find that this last idea isn't really true. Many prisoners are creative and intelligent people—artists, writers, musicians, and craftsmen—who have used their time in prison to develop their skills.

You'll meet some very sad cases. And some tough ones. And you'll meet some very interesting and inspiring people.

The County Jail

If you're waiting to be transferred to federal prison, you may spend some time in a county or local jail. Each local jail is unique, but all are supposed to be inspected by the Federal Bureau of Prisons if they're to be used for federal prisoners. This doesn't mean that county jail is a pleasant place. The food, sanitation, medical care, security, and guards usually are worse than in federal prison. The cells are crowded, often furnished only with bunk beds, dirty blankets, toilet, wash basin, and perhaps a box or table.

Even worse than the dirt may be the atmosphere. Most county jail prisoners are awaiting trial and have no idea when they'll ever be free again. This can be hard on you, as it is on them. Many federal prisoners find their stay in county jail the most depressing of all.

Federal Prison

After you've been sentenced, the Federal Bureau of Prisons determines where you'll be sent. The stated policy is to place a prisoner in the facility nearest his or her home, but you can be sent to any of the 43 federal prisons across the U.S. The U.S. Marshal will then transfer you at a time convenient to his or her office—sometimes weeks after you've begun serving your time.

Federal prisons are so much better than county jails that, at first, you'll think you've entered another world. The food, the living quarters, and the attitude of the officials will all be an improvement.

Admissions and Orientation

The Federal Bureau of Prisons has a uniform national policy on initial processing and orientation of prisoners. Initially, you will be allowed to bring almost nothing with you into prison, except essentials such as glasses and medicine. Usually your clothing will be taken from you and sent to your family. You'll then be fingerprinted, photographed, given an examination for contraband (a "strip search"), a shower, and prison clothing.

You'll then be placed in an "Admissions and Orientation" (A & O) unit for up to several days. You'll be allowed out for meals, exercise, religious services if you wish, and a short haircut. You may not be able to have visitors, and your correspondence may be limited.

The purpose of A & O is to help the prison fit you into their way of life. So you'll spend a lot of time taking medical examinations, educational tests, and interviews with prison educational officers, chaplains, psychiatrists, etc. The purpose of all this testing is to prepare you for "classification."

Classification, which was widely heralded as a reform when the system began, is supposed to provide you with individual treatment and "rehabilitation." Since the only way to rehabilitate you would be to get you to change your CO stand, "individual treatment" doesn't make much sense applied to you—and it may make little more sense applied to other prisoners. The result of the classification procedure is an interview with a "classification board," possibly a lecture on the value of work, and assignment to a prison job.

Prison Life

Daily Routine

The routine within a prison varies from one prison to another. Here's a typical time schedule: 6:15 rising; 6:45 count; 7:00 breakfast; 7:40-11:40 work; 11:50 count; 12:00 lunch; 12:30-4:00 work; 4:30 count; 5:00 supper; 7:30 count; 10:00 lights out. On Saturdays and Sundays there is no work program except for kitchen workers and a few others. Religious services are mostly held on Sundays, although there are sometimes provisions for Jewish, Muslim, and Native American religious practices. Visiting hours vary from prison to prison, usually occurring both during the week and on weekends.

Visits

Visiting privileges are different in each prison. In some places, visiting is restricted to a few hours per week; in others, you'll be able to have visitors every day of the week. The people who can visit you must be on an approved list and are limited to your family and friends as well as visitors from Prisoner Visitation and Support. A guard will supervise the visiting room, but he or she is not supposed to listen to your conversation. You may be subjected to strip searches before and after the visit.

Correspondence

In some prisons, correspondence is limited to an "approved" list of correspondents. In most, though, you'll be able to write and receive letters freely. But your mail may be opened and read by prison officials. At Christmas, you can receive Christmas cards and one holiday gift box.

Work

You'll be assigned to a prison job in an area such as maintenance, industrial jobs like printing, farm work, ditch-digging, or even an office job. Like most prisoners, you'll probably find the work program meaningless, and chances are you won't be very enthusiastic about doing your job. Many war resisters refuse to work in prison industries, or work at all, because they object to the prison system. This can result in your being placed in "administrative segregation," or solitary confinement. It could also lead to your being transferred to a more secure prison.

Medical Service

Medical care varies from prison to prison, but don't count on it being the best. Some prisons have their own hospitals. Others rely on local hospitals.

Chaplains

The prison chaplains conduct religious services, interview prisoners at admission, are available for interviews, and visit prisoners in punishment status or in the hospital. Many chaplains want to help, but they are limited in what they can do. Sometimes, though, a talk with the chaplain may help clear up a problem; and the chaplain can perform minor services like finding a book that you want.

Violence

Violence is common in prison. This isn't surprising. And it can be frightening. Rape does occur, and threats of violence more often than rape. Most COs learn to cope with these threats, but making the adjustment can be hard.

Discipline

Prisons reward obedience by relaxing some of the rules. Favored prisoners get special privileges like better housing, jobs, and more visitors. Prison officials will often overlook rule violations (at least minor ones) by a "good" prisoner. If you defy the system or don't "adjust" to the officials' liking, they can punish you swiftly and sternly. You can be taken before a disciplinary "court" (called the Inmate Disciplinary Committee), which may take your guilt for granted and decide simply how to punish you. You may lose privileges, be placed in solitary confinement, be transferred to a more secure prison, or lose your "good time" (reduction of your sentence earned for good behavior).

Building Your Time

Prisoners have a lot of time on their hands, even with the "work programs" they are forced to take part in. For a prisoner, time is counted not only in months, days, and minutes (two years is 1,051,200 minutes), but in Sunday dinners to be eaten or counts to be endured. Like every other prisoner, you'll have to build your time. That's partly an art and partly a science.

Making your time useful for you—as much as it can be while you're in prison—takes great self-discipline. But resisters who have done it have felt a great sense of freedom for themselves. And they've often been able to help others—for instance, by acting as jailhouse lawyers or by teaching other prisoners to read.

But it's not easy. Many prisoners fall into a routine of going from one escape to another: from work to the television room to the nightly game of chess or bridge to bed, and then again. Prisons destroy initiative and creativity first of all.

You'll meet prisoners whose time has nearly

destroyed them, and prisoners whose lives have changed for the better while they were in prison. The hardest thing about imprisonment is the separation from your loved ones, for you may be far from home. This will put a strain on your relationships which you can overcome only by working hard to do so. Prison will work against all that is best in you. Your best weapons to counter it are personal initiative, physical exercise, a sense of perspective, a sense of humor, and the support of outside friends.

Prisoner Visitation and Support

Sponsored by 35 national religious bodies and socially-concerned agencies, Prisoner Visitation and Support (PVS) seeks to meet the needs of prisoners in the U.S. federal and military prison systems through visits that are separate from official prison structures.

PVS is unique among independent groups because it has access to all U.S. federal and military prisons. The focus of PVS visitors is on those prisoners with a great need for human contact: those serving long sentences, those in solitary confinement, those without visits, and those in maximum-security prisons.

PVS visitors offer friendship, help, and moral support to prisoners. The visitors help prisoners to maintain their self-esteem and support them in their efforts to live constructive lives. They also try to help prisoners who need services not available in prison, like maintaining family ties, writing letters to parole boards, etc.

For further information, contact Prisoner Visitation and Support, 1501 Cherry St., Philadelphia, PA 19102.

PART V

THE UNARMED SOLDIER

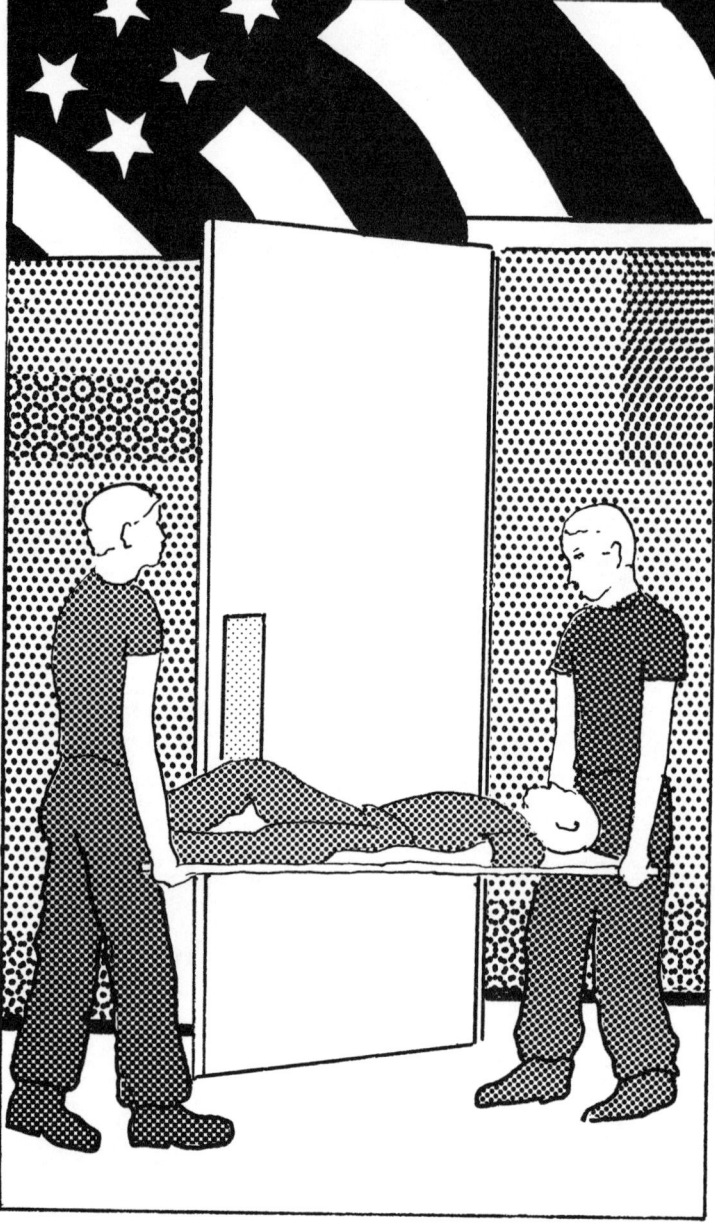

CHAPTER 16
THE UNARMED SOLDIER

On October 12, 1945, President Truman gave the Congressional Medal of Honor to Desmond T. Daws. Daws' citation, listing more than half a dozen acts of heroism on Guam, Leyte, and Okinawa, said he had become a "symbol for outstanding gallantry throughout the 77th Infantry Division." As a member of the 307th Infantry Medical Detachment, Pfc Daws had rescued 75 wounded men from the battlefields in Okinawa.

Daws was a noncombatant conscientious objector. Other unarmed soldiers have received medals for heroism, and COs as a group have received praise from officers and non-commissioned officers in the military who have worked with them.

If you apply for and receive 1-A-0 status, you will be assigned to noncombatant duty in the military. This chapter explains what noncombatants do and what part they play in the military. You should read it if you're thinking about filing for 1-A-0 status, or if you're not sure what status you want.

Training and Duties

Noncombatant duty for conscientious objectors in the armed forces was defined by the President in

Executive Order No. 10028 (January 13, 1949), as follows:

- service in any unit of the armed forces which is unarmed at all times;
- service in the medical department of any of the armed forces, wherever performed; or
- any other assignment the primary function of which does not require the use of arms in combat; provided that such other assignment is acceptable to the individual concerned and does not require him to bear arms or be trained in their use.

The term "noncombatant training" means any training which is not concerned with the study, use, or handling of arms or weapons. Department of Defense Directive 1300.6 (Conscientious Objectors in the Armed Forces), paragraph III, C, 4, states, "Service aboard an armed ship or aircraft or in a combat zone shall not be considered to be combatant duty unless the individual concerned is personally and directly involved in the operation of weapons."

If you were drafted as a 1-A-0, you would receive basic training much like a combatant soldier. The difference would be that you wouldn't be required to train with or use weapons. Most 1-A-0 soldiers receive training as medics after they have completed basic training. But this doesn't always happen. Noncombatant soldiers have worked as chaplain's assistants, company clerks, and even shipping clerks.

Chances are, though, that you'd be a medic. The Army gives medics a ten-week course which trains them for three related types of assignment: hospital orderly, dispensary attendant, and field medic. Among the skills taught are emergency medical treatment and symptom recognition. In addition to classroom instruction, there are many hours of out-of-doors training in preparing splints and bandaging, setting up a medical tent, carrying wounded on a stretcher, carrying wounded without a stretcher, ambulance and helicopter loading of casualties, and various other practical exercises. A good part of one week is spent learning how to give injections.

Only a few medics are COs. Many non-CO medics enlisted for the medical corps and after their first medic training will receive additional training as medical specialists. A few 1-A-0s with special aptitudes or experience may also receive such training.

A medical specialist is often the direct supervisor of medical corpsmen, and among the things he or she learns are basic anatomy and physiology, casualty evacuation, and general principles of nursing.

When all training is complete, medics are sent to a permanent station in the U.S. or overseas. There is absolutely nothing in the regulations to prevent a CO from being sent to a war zone. 1-A-0 medics were among the first draftees sent to Vietnam.

Mission of the Army Medical Service

"The Army Medical Service supports all elements of the Army and is primarily concerned with maintaining the health and fighting efficiency of the individual soldier."

This statement from the Army Field Manual (FM) 8-10 (Medical Support, Theater of Operations, April, 1970, para. 2-1) is perfectly logical. The purpose of armies in combat is to win military victories. Every part of the military helps to do this. Some people accept noncombatant service thinking the medics are instruments of mercy. This idea can lead to serious personal problems. Medics do save lives and ease suffering. But the medic is a member of the armed forces, and the goal of the members is to win battles.

This point is made again and again in FM 8-10, which outlines the work of medics in combat areas. Saving lives and easing suffering are not even mentioned as part of the mission of the medics.

The Manual states, "The mission of the Army Medical Department in a theater of operations is to conserve the fighting strength of the Army by recommending, supervising, and implementing measures for safeguarding the health of the troops through effective medical care and treatment, rapid and orderly evacuation of the sick and wounded, and early return of patients to duty" (para. 2-1).

Injured soldiers are to be treated, not for their health, but for military necessity: "The objective of hospitalization is to return sick or injured personnel to duty as rapidly as possible. Because of their training and experience, they are the most valuable of all replacements" (para. 7-1).

When the available medical resources are limited, this consideration is most important. "Since the objective of military medicine is to conserve trained manpower, medical resources must be employed to do the most good for the greatest number. When a wide disparity exists between requirements (i.e., the number of wounded) and available means [of caring for them], it may be necessary to favor those patients who can be returned to immediate duty, rather than those more seriously injured" (para 2-6).

Para. 7-1 also states that "under combat conditions, medical means must be distributed in order to provide the greatest service to the greatest number. To devote a disproportionate amoung of time and effort to one patient at the expense of the treatment of the majority is to subordinate the common welfare of many to one."

Even when casualties are evacuated from the combat zone to a field hospital or medical unit, "No patient is evacuated further to the rear than his physical condition warrants or the military situation requires. The evacuation policy of the command designates a maximum period of time during which patients may be retained for treatment within the command prior to being returned to duty" (para. 2-5).

Discharge and Transfer

DoD Directive 1300.6 provides for discharge of conscientious objectors or their transfer to noncombatant status. The standards which COs in the military have to meet are the same as those explained in Chapter 5.

If you're in the military and want a discharge or transfer, you should get a copy of CCCO's *Advice for Conscientious Objectors in the Armed Forces*. You should also get counseling because the procedures for discharge or transfer are complicated. CCCO can help you find a counselor.

If you apply for 1-A-0 status under the draft and are drafted as a noncombatant, you may find that you object to what you're required to do in the military. There's nothing to stop you from applying for discharge and getting it, and many unhappy 1-A-0s have been discharged as 1-0 conscientious objectors. You'll need counseling, though. You'll have to apply to the military just like a combatant soldier. The fact that your draft board recognized your 1-A-0 claim may help you get a discharge because it helps to show that you're sincere. But the military may give you trouble for a lot of reasons. They may wonder why you changed your mind. They may tell you there's nothing you can do. Or they just may not want to lose a useful soldier.

It's best to decide before you're in the military rather than after.

Which Status for You?

Most COs take the 1-0 position. But if you object to killing and don't object to being part of the military, the 1-A-0 stand is the one that fits you. Keep in mind, though, that when you're part of the military, you're part of the military. You're not "special," except that you can't be ordered to use weapons. You get military training, and you're part of the military mission.

How do you feel about this? If you have any objection at all to it, you should apply for 1-0 status.

APPENDICES

QUESTIONS ASKED COs

You will be asked many questions at your personal appearance. Your local board or the appeal board may be hostile, straightforward, friendly, or apparently friendly but actually bent on tripping you up.

Your answers should be straightforward and sincere. You don't have to give detailed, logical answers. You may never be able to convince the questioner that you are right, but you may be able to convince him or her that you're sincere. Often the way you answer the question is as important as the answer you give. Keep in mind that you are trying to get across the fact that because of your beliefs you can't take part in war. So stick to that subject. Don't spend too much time talking about things not directly related to your beliefs.

The questions below are real. They have been asked, along with thousands of others. You won't be asked all of them, and you may be asked some which aren't even hinted at here. The questions you get asked will depend on your background, the answers you give (including your written CO statement), which CO status you are seeking, and the character of the questioner.

If you have a friend or counselor ask you these questions and any others he or she can think up, you'll be better prepared to face your personal appearance. And going over these questions before you prepare your CO statement may help to make your own thinking more clear.

Nature of Belief

Do you doubt that God exists?
Is your conscientious objection to war deeply rooted in your own free thinking and personal opinions?
How can you say that your belief is religious?
Is your objection to killing or being killed?
What does your church say about war?
Why do most members of your church support military force?
Where in the Bible do you find anything which forbids you to defend your country?

Why did Christ say, "He that hath no sword, let him buy one," "Render unto Caesar that which is Caesar's," and "I came not to bring peace, but a sword"?

What would you do if God told you to defend your country?

How about the Christian doctrine of approval for just wars?

How do you explain all the wars in the Old Testament?

Do you think America's millions who killed and died in wars were immoral to kill?

Is it ever an honor to die for your country if you die keeping the enemy from conquering it?

Do you think that combat soldiers who believe they serve God in serving their country are misled?

Can no war be just and necessary regardless of the situation?

Do you believe in Romans 13:1-8 of the New Testament, in which it states that God ordains the governing authorities to be servants of God for the good of the governed?

Is there any possibility at all that your CO application comes out of a feeling of uncertainty, insecurity, or fear of military hardships?

Why aren't there any atheists in foxholes?

Why Not 1-A-0?

Does God love that dying American infantry soldier on the battlefield? Would he want someone like you to try to save his life? Does "loving one's neighbor as oneself" ever include being a medic?

Would it be a high honor for you to die for our country if you did so while helping to save the life of a dying American soldier?

Can you say that a medic helping a dying soldier is an immoral act and can never be an expression of God's love?

If you don't believe in killing, why let a wounded soldier die?

How, When, and From Whom or What Source?

Do you respect and follow the religion of your parents?

Did you arrive at your decision to apply for CO by your own personal ideas alone?

Did books you read have most to do with influencing your request for CO status?

Since you say you have been a CO for only two months, might your conscience not change back again two months from now?

Who helped you prepare your CO application? Are these really your *own* beliefs?

Use of Force

Do you honestly think the Armed Forces should be abolished?

What method would you use to resist evil?
Would you forcibly restrain individual law breakers?
Would you use force to preserve anything you believe in?
Would you use force to prevent a maniac from killing an innocent person?
From killing you?
From killing himself?
Wasn't Hitler a maniac?
Can't non-physical force, such as strikes and boycotts, be just as painful and destructive as physical violence?
If someone were attacking your mother, would you try to stop him or would you call the police?
Didn't Jesus use violence in driving the money changers from the temple?
Do you think that the federal government was right in using military force as it has in riots, disorders, and racial strife?
Do you think blacks are justified in using self-defense?
Do you believe in the kind of force the police often have to use to stop killer criminals from murdering others?

What Have You Done?

Are you trying to influence others to become conscientious objectors?
How can you *prove* that you're a CO?
What will you do if your application is denied?

And Some Other Questions

Aren't there a lot of Communists mixed up in so-called peace demonstrations?
What happens to people like you in Russia or China?
If everyone held your view, wouldn't the Communists take over the country?
Why do you take your place in a society organized by force and then refuse to fight its wars?
Why do you pay taxes?
If you really believe these things, why can't you just go into the military and then write a book or speak out about your beliefs? Wouldn't people have more respect for what you have to say knowing that you have served your country?
Aren't you bringing a great deal of dishonor on your family?
Do you think that the authority of your conscience is much more reliable than the consciences of most Americans?
Do you realize that you are helping to destroy this society?

FURTHER READING

There are many books on conscientious objection, war, and non-violence. The list below is only a sample. It has been designed to include books which you can find easily, either in a bookstore or in the library. Where a book is marked OP, it is out of print, but should be available in the library. Books marked PB are available in paperback.

War in Literature

Bates, Scott. *Poems of War Resistance*. New York: Grossman Publishers, 1969. OP

A beautiful collection of poems from 2300 BC to the present.

Brittain, Vera. *Testament of Youth*. New York: Wideview Books, 1980.

Powerful autobiography by a major British anti-war activist. Shows World War I as seen by a nurse who worked at the front lines.

Camus, Albert. *The Myth of Sisyphus*. New York: Alfred A. Knopf, 1955. PB: New York: Random House/Vintage, 1959.

Philosophical thoughts on life, war, suicide, and absurdity.

cummings, e. e. *The Enormous Room*. New York: Liveright, 1970. PB available.

An account of the prison experiences of the poet who, with a friend, was arrested by the French government while serving as an ambulance driver during World War I.

Hasek, Jaroslav. *The Good Soldier Schweik,* trans. by Paul Selver. New York: Signet, 1963. PB

Hasek, who fought in World War I, exposes the folly of war and the military and gives the reader a good laugh as well. Schweik never quite fits into the army because he does what comes naturally to him instead of what he is told.

Heller, Joseph. *Catch-22*. New York: Simon & Schuster, 1961. PB available.

Set in World War II, this is the best modern satire on war and the military.

Hemingway, Ernest. *A Farewell to Arms*. New York: Scribner's, 1929.

One of the great war novels, this tells the story of an ambulance driver on the Italian front in World War I and the woman he loved.

Hersey, John. *The War Lover*. New York: Alfred A. Knopf, 1959.

Set in World War II, this is a gripping story of one bomber pilot's discovery of his own destructiveness.

Mowat, Farley. *And No Birds Sang*. Boston: Atlantic Monthly Press, 1979.

A powerful story of what it was like to be a Canadian infantryman in Italy during World War II. Mowat, best known for his nature books, says he could not bring himself to write this book for thirty-five years. May be the best anti-war book published in the last ten years.

Parsons, I. M. *Men Who March Away: Poems of the First World War*. New York: The Viking Press, 1965.

A good selection of poems by the men in the trenches (Wilfred Owen, Siegfried Sassoon, etc.) and civilians who saw the war from England. Grueling reading, especially the trenches poems.

Remarque, Erich Maria. *All Quiet on the Western Front*, trans. by A. W. Wheen. Boston: Little, Brown, 1929. PB: Greenwich, Ct.: Fawcett, 1978.

This classic novel shows World War I from a German enlisted soldier's point of view. The combat scenes are especially well-done.

Rottmann, Larry, Jan Barry, and Basil T. Pacquet (eds.) *Winning Hearts and Minds: War Poems by Vietnam Veterans*. New York: East River Press, 1977. PB

A moving and chilling book of poems by men who were in the Vietnam War.

Sassoon, Siegfried. *Memoirs of an Infantry Officer*. Riverside, N.J.: MacMillan, 1969. PB available.

No-nonsense autobiographical story of World War I by an

anti-war poet who was an officer in the trenches. Pulls no punches on war, military incompetence, etc.

Tolstoy, Leo. *War and Peace*. Available in many editions and translations.

Considered by some the greatest novel ever written, this is an account of Napoleon's invasion of Russia, and much, much more. Tolstoy not only tells the story but reflects on war, fate, and history.

Trumbo, Dalton. *Johnny Got His Gun*. New York: Bantam Books, 1978. PB

This powerful novel tells of a war veteran who was wounded in combat and has lost his arms, legs, eyes, and ability to speak. One of the most famous anti-war books.

Vonnegut, Kurt, Jr. *Slaughterhouse Five*. New York: Delacorte Press, 1969. PB available.

Vonnegut's only war novel tells the story of Billy Pilgrim, who was a prisoner of war caught in the firebombing of Dresden in World War II. The author was also a POW and actually saw the destruction of Dresden.

Wyndham, John. *Re-Birth*. New York: Ballantine Books, 1978. PB

This well-done science fiction story shows the world as it might be after a nuclear war. Life is primitive, and large parts of the earth are blasted and so radioactive that no one dares go there.

War in History

Barbeau, Arthur, and Forette Henri. *The Unknown Soldiers: Black American Troops in World War I*. Philadelphia: Temple University Press, 1974.

A well-researched history of black soldiers and the mistreatment they found in the World War I military.

Fay, Sidney B. *The Origins of the World War*. Riverside, N.J.: MacMillan, 1959. PB: Free Press, 1967.

First published in 1930, this was the earliest book to argue that the Germans were not solely responsible for World War I.

Knightly, Phillip. *The First Casualty: From the Crimea to Vietnam: The War Correspondent as Hero, Propagandist, and Myth Maker*. New York and London: Harcourt, Brace, Janovich, 1975. PB available.

This lively book tells how, since about 1850, newspaper and

broadcast reporters have covered wars. It shows how the war correspondents have been used by the government and the military and how censorship has sometimes made good reporting impossible.

Lafore, Laurence. *The End of Glory: An Interpretation of the Origins of World War II*. Philadelphia and New York: J. B. Lippincott, 1970. PB available.

A careful treatment of the roots of the Second World War, this book traces the war's origins to the breakdown of the old order in Europe beginning before World War I.

Motley, Mary Penick. *The Invisible Soldier: The Experience of the Black Soldier, World War II*. Detroit: Wayne State University Press, 1975.

An oral history of the troubles of black soldiers in World War II. Will surprise a lot of readers.

Mullen, R. W. *Blacks in America's Wars*. New York: Monad Press, 1973. PB: Pathfinder Press, 1974.

Covers the experience of black troops in wars from the Revolution to Vietnam.

Stone, I. F. *The Hidden History of the Korean War*. New York: Monthly Review Press, 1969. PB only.

America's leading independent radical journalist argues that we have never been given the full story of the United Nations' "police action" in Korea.

Swomley, John M., Jr. *American Empire: The Political Ethics of Twentieth-Century Conquest*. Riverside, N.J.: MacMillan, 1970. PB available.

One of the best overall introductions to recent foreign policy and the myths that have grown up around it. Readable and thought-provoking.

Taylor, A. J. P. *The Origins of the Second World War*. New York: Atheneum, 1961 (OP). PB: Greenwich, Ct.: Fawcett, 1961.

A well-known historian argues that the Allies deserve some of the blame for World War II.

Modern War and Its Victims

Branfman, Fred. *Voices from the Plain of Jars: Life Under an Air War*. New York: Harper & Row, 1972. OP

This collection of essays and drawings by Laotian peasants shows the destruction and misery caused by the bombing of Laos.

Calder, Nigel. *Nuclear Nightmares: An Investigation into Possible Wars.* New York: Viking Press, 1980.

This sobering book tries to show how a nuclear war might begin. It explores five different possible wars.

Hersey, John. *Hiroshima.* New York: Alfred A. Knopf, 1969.

A powerful report on six survivors of the Hiroshima bombing and what they went through when the bomb hit.

Irving, David. *The Destruction of Dresden.* New York: Holt, Rinehart & Winston, 1963. OP

Late in World War II, Allied bombers firebombed Germany's most cultured city, killing more people than died in Hiroshima and Nagasaki combined. This is a good history of that terrible night.

Kovic, Ron. *Born on the Fourth of July.* New York: McGraw-Hill, 1976. PB: Pocket Books, 1978.

Autobiography of a wounded and paralyzed Vietnam veteran who joined the anti-war movement. Kovic spares the reader none of his pain.

War and Politics

Barnet, Richard J. *The Giants: Russia and America.* New York: Simon & Schuster, 1977. PB available.

This history of Soviet-American relations traces the conflict between the two to troubles at home on both sides.

The Boston Study Group. *The Price of Defense: A New Strategy for Military Spending.* New York: Times Books, 1979.

A well-researched case for a smaller military budget, both to save money and to help end the arms race.

Klare, Michael T. *War Without End: American Planning for the Next Vietnams.* New York: Alfred A. Knopf, 1972. PB: Random House/Vintage, 1972.

Klare shows that the American policies which led to Vietnam have actually changed very little. A difficult but revealing book.

Lens, Sidney. *The Day Before Doomsday.* Garden City, N.Y.: Doubleday, 1977.

A detailed treatment of the nuclear arms race which shows how it can lead to nuclear war.

The Causes of War

Barnet, Richard J. *The Economy of Death.* New York: Atheneum, 1969. PB available.

The author, who has written many books and articles on the Cold War, here looks at the military-industrial complex and what can be done about it.

Blainey, Geoffrey. *The Causes of War.* New York: The Free Press, 1973.

This challenging attempt to find common roots for all wars argues that war and peace are part of the same international system. Blainey believes that wars occur when nations "agree" to fight.

Lorenz, Konrad. *On Aggression.* New York: Harcourt, Brace & World, 1966. PB: Harcourt, Brace, Janovich, 1974.

Lorenz, who is famous for his animal studies, here traces the roots of war to a human "killer instinct."

Montagu, M. F. Ashley. *The Nature of Human Aggression.* New York: Oxford University Press, 1976. PB: New York: Oxford, 1978.

A well-known anthropologist argues that there is no human "killer instinct."

Conscientious Objection

Bainton, Roland H. *Christian Attitudes Toward War and Peace: A Historical Survey and Critical Re-Evaluation.* New York: Abingdon Press, 1960. PB available.

The author examines the writings of the church fathers and evolving Christian attitudes toward participation in war, showing how Christians came to terms with the state.

Berrigan, Daniel. *No Bars to Manhood.* Garden City, N.Y.: Doubleday, 1970. PB: Bantam, 1971. OP

Berrigan, a noted anti-war figure, traces the influences on his thinking from his days as chaplain at Cornell to his draft file destruction at Catonsville, Md.

Brock, Peter. *History of Pacifism in the United States from the Colonial Era to the First World War.* Princeton, N.J.: Princeton University Press, 1968. PB available.

The most complete study of conscientious objection in all American wars through World War I. Includes a wealth of stories about Quakers, Garrisonians, and others as conscientious objectors and peace activists.

.... *Twentieth-Century Pacifism.* New York: Van Nostrand, Reinhold, 1970. PB available.

Traces pacifism and conscientious objection through the great and small wars of this century.

Finn, James (ed.) *A Conflict of Loyalties: The Case for Selective Conscientious Objection.* New York: Pegasus, 1968.

A collection of essays that present the case for objection to a particular war.

Harris, David. *Goliath.* New York: Sidereal Press, 1970.

Harris, former husband of Joan Baez and a well-known draft resister, here writes his reflections on war, America, prison, etc.

Hesse, Hermann. *If the War Goes On ... Reflections on War and Politics*, trans. by Ralph Manheim. New York: Farrar, Straus and Giroux, 1971.

The Nobel-Prize-winning novelist was also an outspoken pacifist. These beautifully written essays present his position. Hesse emphasizes the need for each person to choose.

McSorley, Richard. *New Testament Basis of Peacemaking.* Washington, D.C.: Center for Peace Studies, Georgetown University, 1979.

A detailed discussion of the New Testament's teachings on war.

Mayer, Peter (ed.) *The Pacifist Conscience.* New York: Holt, Rinehart & Winston, 1966. OP

Alternatives to violence from early times to the present. Contains an excellent reading list.

Muste, A. J. *Essays*, ed. by Nat Hentoff. Indianapolis: Bobbs-Merrill, 1967. PB: Simon & Schuster/Touchstone, 1970.

A collection of the most important writings by one of this century's best-known pacifists.

National Interreligious Service Board for Conscientious Objectors. *Words of Conscience: Religious Statements on Conscientious Objection.* Washington: NISBCO, 1980.

The best collection of official church statements—including Native American, Nation of Islam, etc.—on conscientious objection. (Available from NISBCO, 550 Washington Bldg., 15th & New York Ave., NW, Washington, DC 20005.)

Schlissel, Lillian (ed.) *Conscience in America.* New York: Dutton, 1968. PB available.

A documentary history of conscientious objection in America, this is a good collection of historic documents, both well- and little-known.

Thoreau, Henry David. "On the Duty of Civil Disobedience." In *Walden and Other Writings.* Garden City, N.Y.: Doubleday, 1970. (Many other editions.)

The basic text on civil disobedience and resistance to unjust laws. Influenced Gandhi, draft resistance, etc.

Yoder, John H. *The Politics of Jesus.* Grand Rapids, Mich.: Wm. B. Eerdmans Pub. Co., 1972.

Thought-provoking group of essays by a well-known Mennonite theologian.

Zahn, Gordon C. *Another Part of the War: The Camp Simon Story.* Amherst, Mass.: University of Massachusetts Press, 1979.

The well-known Catholic sociologist and pacifist gives a history and personal account of Camp Simon, a CO camp in World War II, and reflects on the meaning of the experience.

Non-Violence

Bondurant, Joan. *The Conquest of Violence.* Berkeley, Ca.: University of California Press, 1965. PB available.

A study of the philosophy and strategy of Gandhian non-violent direct action.

del Vasto, Lanza. *Warriors of Peace: Writings on the Technique of Nonviolence.* New York: Alfred A. Knopf, 1974. PB available.

The leader of the French non-violent movement here gives his thoughts on war, peace, and non-violent action.

Gregg, Richard. *The Power of Non-Violence.* New York: Schocken, 1959. 2nd Ed.: Nyack, N.Y.: Fellowship, 1959. PB: Schocken, 1959.

The classic treatment of Gandhi's non-violent philosophy and its relation to non-violence in the West.

Hallie, Philip. *Lest Innocent Blood Be Shed: The Story of the Village of Le Chambon and How Goodness Happened There.* New York: Harper & Row, 1979. PB available.

The amazing history of how one French village organized, quietly and non-violently, to save the lives of thousands of Jews during World War II.

Jewish Peace Fellowship. *The Roots of Jewish Nonviolence.* Nyack, N.Y.: Jewish Peace Fellowship.

A collection of articles on Jewish opposition to war.

Jezer, Marty, Cooney, Robert, and Helen Michalowski. *The Power of the People: Active Nonviolence in the United States.* Culver City, Ca.: Peace Press, 1977.

Well-done picture history of the nonviolent movements in the United States.

King, Martin Luther, Jr. *The Trumpet of Conscience.* New York: Harper & Row, 1968.

The civil rights leader and Nobel Peace Prize winner's last book covers non-violence and social change, Vietnam, and other topics. A beautiful Christmas sermon on peace ends the book.

Lakey, George. *Strategy for a Living Revolution.* New York: Grossman Publishers, 1973.

A major work on non-violent methods for gaining social justice.

Lynd, Staughton (ed.) *Non-Violence in America: A Documentary History.* Indianapolis, Ind.: Bobbs-Merrill, 1966. PB available.

A good collection of essays on American non-violence.

Merton, Thomas. *Faith and Violence.* South Bend, Ind.: Notre Dame Press, 1968. PB available.

In a series of essays written during the Vietnam War, the author discusses war, revolution, and Christian action.

Merton, Thomas (ed.) *Gandhi on Non-Violence.* New York: New Directions, 1965. PB available.

A collection of quotes from Gandhi edited by the late Trappist monk and leading exponent of non-violence.

Stanford, Barbara (ed.) *Peace Making: A Guide to Conflict Resolution.* New York: Bantam, 1976. PB

A collection of practical essays on non-violent solutions to conflict.

Tolstoy, Leo. *The Kingdom of God Is Within You,* trans. by Leo Weiner. New York: Farrar, Straus and Cudahy, 1961. PB

An interpretation of the Sermon on the Mount, this is the major statement of Tolstoy's belief in non-violence.

Films

Many feature films on war present alternatives to the usual viewpoints. A sampling of these films appears below. These may appear on television or come to a neighborhood theater.

All Quiet on the Western Front (the 1930s version starring Lew Ayres)

Although a new version has been made for television, the original film, which won an Oscar as best picture, is well worth seeing. It includes some philosophical and humorous discussion of the causes of war and the follies of rulers. The ending is one of the most famous in film history.

All Quiet on the Western Front (the made-for-television version starring Richard Thomas and Ernest Borgnine)

One of the strongest anti-war statements ever shown on network television, this film, like the original version, shows the horrors of war in striking detail. The battle scenes are grueling to watch, partly because the Czech government donated a village, soon to be torn down anyway, which was leveled by artillery fire during the filming.

A Bridge Too Far (all-star cast including Liv Ullman, Lord Olivier, Robert Redford, and Sean Connery)

Intended by producer Joseph E. Levine as an anti-war statement, this film portrays the Allied operation at Arnhem, Holland, in 1944. The operation was a disaster for military and civilians alike. Excellent, harrowing battle footage leads to a moving ending showing the plight of war's victims—civilian and military.

Coming Home (starring Jane Fonda and Jon Voight)

This portrayal of the relationship between a wounded Vietnam veteran and a soldier's wife makes a strong statement about Vietnam and all wars. Most people who were in the anti-Vietnam movement like it better than other films such as *The Deer Hunter*.

The King of Hearts (starring Alan Bates and Genevieve Bujold; directed by Phillipe deBroca)

A fine World War I satire that raises the question whether "sane" people who fight in wars are really sane at all.

SOME GROUPS WORKING FOR PEACE

American Friends Service Committee, 1501 Cherry St., Philadelphia, Pa. 19102.

Amnesty International, 2112 Broadway, New York, NY 10023

Center for War/Peace Studies, 218 E. 18th St., New York, NY 10003

Clergy and Laity Concerned, 198 Broadway, New York, NY 10038

Fellowship of Reconciliation, Box 271, Nyack, NY 10960

Friends Committee on National Legislation, 245 Second St., NE, Washington, DC 20002

National Interreligious Service Board for Conscientious Objectors, 15th & New York Ave., NW, Washington, DC 20005

SANE: A Citizens' Committee for a Sane World, 318 Massachusetts Ave., NE, Washington, DC 20002

Society for Social Responsibility in Science, 221 Rock Hill Rd., Bala Cynwyd, Pa. 19004

Southern Christian Leadership Conference, 334 Auburn Ave., NE, Atlanta, Ga. 30303

War Resisters League, 339 Lafayette St., New York, NY 10012

Women's International League for Peace and Freedom, 1213 Race St., Philadelphia, Pa. 19107

NOTES ON SOURCES

Chapter 1

p. 1: The trial of Maximilianus is taken from Peter Mayer (ed.), *The Pacifist Conscience* (New York: Holt, Rinehart, Winston, 1966), pp. 328-329.

p. 1: World War II soldiers who did not fire at the enemy: Survey reported by Brig. Gen. S. L. A. Marshall, *Men Against Fire*, William Morrow, 1947. Quoted in John Keegan, "Men in Battle," *Human Nature*, Vol. I, No. 6 (June, 1978), p. 36.

p. 2: Greek COs were covered in several articles in *CCCO News Notes*. See Vol. 29, No. 1, No. 2, No. 3; Vol. 30, No. 1.

Chapter 2

p. 7: Recruitment figures are from *America's Volunteers* (December 31, 1978), a study prepared for the Department of Defense, p. 190.

Chapter 3

Principle sources for this chapter were the Military Selective Service Act (1971) and final Selective Service Regulations published in the Federal Register for February 1, 1982 (Vol. 47, No. 21), pp. 4640-4665.

Chapter 4

Principle Sources for this chapter were the Military Selective Service Act (1971) and Presidential Proclamation 4771, July 2, 1980.

Chapter 5

The major cases on conscientious objection are *U.S. v. Seeger*, 380 US 163 (1965); *Welsh v. U.S.*, 398 US 333 (1970); *Sicurella v. U.S.*, 348 US 385 (1955); *Gillette v. U.S.*, 401 US 437 (1971);

In re Nissen, 146 F.Supp. 361 (1956); *In re Hansen*, 148 F.Supp. 187 (1957); and *Fleming v. U.S.*, 344 F.2d 912 (10th Cir. 1965).

p. 54: *Clay v. U.S.*, 403 US 698 (1971)

pp. 55-56: Quote from Paul Tillich cited in *U.S. v. Seeger*. Quote from John Woolman is from Reginald Reynolds (ed.), *The Wisdom of John Woolman* (London: George Allen & Unwin, 1948), p. 105. Quote from Martin Luther King is from M. L. King, *The Trumpet of Conscience* (New York: Harper & Row, 1967), p. 69. Quote from David Saville Muzzey cited in *Seeger*.

p. 56: On the importance of individual beliefs, see *U.S. v. Seeger*.

p. 56: On religious training, see *Nissen and Hansen*.

p. 57: On the use of force, see *U.S. v. Purvis*, 403 F.2d 555 (2d Cir. 1968); see also *Gillette*.

p. 57: "real shooting wars": *Sicurella v. U.S.*

p. 58: Quote on "deeply held" beliefs from *Kemp v. Bradley*, 457 F.2d 627 (8th Cir. 1972).

p. 59: On "political" beliefs, see *Fleming v. U.S.*; see also *Welsh v. U.S.* and *U.S. v. Seeger*.

p. 60: On sincerity, see *Bates v. Commander, First Coast Guard District*, 413 F.2d 475 (1st Cir. 1969), here quoted; see also *U.S. v. James*, 417 F.2d 826 (4th Cir. 1969); *U.S. v. Hesse*, 417 F.2d 141 (8th Cir. 1969); and *U.S. v. Martin*, 416 F.2d 44 (10th Cir. 1969).

p. 61: On 1-O and 1-A-O status there are two important cases: *U.S. v. Relyea* (1953), an unpublished case from the Northern District of Ohio; and *U.S. v. Carson*, 282 F.Supp. 261 (E.D. Ark. 1968). *Relyea* held that 1-A-O cannot be given as a "compromise." *Carson* held that a local board could give one classification even though the other was requested, if the board found that the registrant really qualified for the other classification. Carson had requested 1-A-O status and received it; the court held that his claim qualified him for 1-O status, and he should have been given this classification.

Chapter 6

p. 63: On COs under the World War II English draft, see Denis Hayes, *Challenge of Conscience* (London: George Allen & Unwin, 1949). On pre-Vietnam discussions about selective objection, see Richard J. Niebanck, *Conscience, War, and the Selective Objector* (Board of Social Ministry, Lutheran Church in America), pp. 40-41.

p. 64: I am grateful to Dr. Mark Sakharov for his thoughts on counter insurgency war and other issues in "The Draftee and Modern War," an unpublished paper which he shared with me.

p. 64: Quotation is from *Gillette v. U.S.*

p. 65: On past wars, see *U.S. v. Stewart*, 6 SSLR 3255 (2nd Cir. 1973); and *U.S. v. Willson*, 452 F.2d 529 (9th Cir. 1971).

pp. 66-68: Niebanck, pp. 39-41, summarizes the just war theory.

A full treatment of the theory will be found in Roland H. Bainton, *Christian Attitudes Toward War and Peace* (New York: Abingdon Press, 1960).

p. 67: *U.S. v. Berg*, 310 F.Supp. 1157 (D.Me. 1970).

Chapter 7

This chapter is based on my own analysis and counseling experience and that of others at CCCO.

Chapter 8

This chapter is based on the Military Selective Service Act and on the Selective Service proposal cited in the text. The World War II British alternative service program is detailed in Denis Hayes, *Challenge of Conscience*, cited above.

Chapter 9

This chapter represents my own conclusions. General sources and ideas for further study are given below.

p. 97: On war and arms races: Laurence Lafore, in *The Long Fuse: An Interpretation of the Origins of the First World War* (Philadelphia and New York: Lippincott, 1965), p. 189, states flatly that arms races in themselves do not cause wars. A thorough analysis of the pressures and interests which lie behind the current arms race will be found in Alva Myrdal, *The Game of Disarmament* (New York: Pantheon Books, 1976).

pp. 97-98: The discussion of U.S. war plans is based on press reports.

p. 98: There is no standard one-volume history of World War I. A good short history, written from a military commander's point of view, is B. H. Liddell Hart, *The Real War, 1914-1918* (Boston: Little, Brown & Co., 1930). More readable but less complete is Alan Lloyd, *The War in the Trenches* (New York: David McKay, 1976).

p. 98: John Keegan, "Men in Battle," cited above, contains a discussion of drilled warfare.

p. 100: An excellent source of information on modern "conventional" weapons is National Action and Research on the Military-Industrial Complex (NARMIC), 1500 Race St., Philadelphia, Pa. 19102. On chemical and biological warfare, see Seymour Hersh, *Chemical and Biological Warfare* (Indianapolis, Ind.: Bobbs-Merrill, 1968).

p. 102: On the laws of war, see Tom J. Farer, *The Laws of War 25 Years After Nuremberg*, Carnegie Endowment for International Peace pamphlet 583, May 1971.

p. 102: On military members' right to refuse unlawful orders, see Stichman & Rivkin, *The Rights of Military Personnel* (New York: Avon, 1977), pp. 103-104.

p. 104: An interesting discussion of total war will be found in Raymond Aron, *The Century of Total War* (Garden City, NY: Doubleday, 1954).

p. 105: A discussion of Sherman's March to the Sea from a military viewpoint will be found in B. H. Liddell Hart, *Strategy: The Indirect Approach* (New York: Praeger, 1954), pp. 151-153. Documents on Sherman's operation are reprinted in Paul M. Angle and Earl Schenck Miers (eds.), *Tragic Years: 1860-1865* (New York: Simon & Schuster, 1960), Vol. II, pp. 924-948.

p. 106: A good introduction to the subject of guerilla warfare is Francois Sully, *Age of the Guerilla: The New Warfare* (New York: Parents Magazine Press, 1968).

p. 107: Books on combat are many, some excellent, some almost useless. This discussion is based on first-hand accounts in Erich Maria Remarque, *All Quiet on the Western Front*, trans. by A. W. Wheen (Boston: Little, Brown, 1929); Farley Mowat, *And No Birds Sang* (Boston: Atlantic Monthly Press, 1979); and Siegfried Sassoon, *Memoirs of an Infantry Officer* (Riverside, N.J.: MacMillan, 1969). A good analysis of combat and human psychology will be found in John Keegan, "Men in Battle," cited above. Keegan's book, *The Face of Battle* (New York: Vintage Books, 1977), is harder going but worth reading. A good introduction to the "art of war" as seen by commanders is B. H. Liddell Hart, *Strategy: The Indirect Approach*, cited above. The discussion on military training and its effects is based on conversations with many military personnel while counseling them.

pp. 109-110: The quote on the Verdun battlefield is from Alistair Horne, *The Price of Glory: Verdun 1916* (Middlesex, Eng.: Penguin Books, 1964), pp. 187-188. The World War II quote is from Farley Mowat, *And No Birds Sang*, pp. 205-206.

p. 110: Statistics on military spending are approximations from the Stockholm Institute for Peace Research.

pp. 110-111: The quote on militarism is from Sidney B. Fay, *The Origins of the World War* (New York: MacMillan, 1928, 1930), p. 39. Definitions not in quotes are from Webster's Unabridged Dictionary.

p. 111: The literature on the causes of war would fill a library of its own. Some suggested readings will be found under "Further Reading."

Chapter 10

p. 113: Casualty figures for nearly all wars are estimates only. For the Thirty Years War, see Field Marshall Viscount Montgomery of Alamein, *A History of Warfare* (Cleveland and New York: World Publishing Co., 1968), p. 279. Civil War figures are official statistics, quoted in Roger Parkinson, *The Encyclopedia of Modern War* (New York: Stein and Day, 1977), p. 7. The ten million figure for World War I is from E. L. Bogart, *Direct and Indirect Costs of the Great War* (1920), quoted in C. R. M. F. Crutwell, *A History of the Great War* (Oxford: The Clarendon Press, 1934), p. 630. World War II figures do not include concentration camp victims. They are taken from Parkinson, p. 149. The Hiroshima figure is from Parkinson, p. 78.

p. 113: Nuclear casualty figure from Maj. Thad A. Wolfe, "Soviet-United States Civil Defense: Tipping the Strategic Scale?", *Air University Review*, March/April, 1979, p. 41.

pp. 113-114: The discussion of the effects of nuclear war is based on Wolfe and on a study by the U.S. government reported in May, 1979. "Civil Defense Scenario Imagines Life After A-Bombing," *Washington Post*, May 23, 1979, p. 2. The figure on the size of the U.S. arsenal is from Sidney Lens, "The Doomsday Strategy," *The Progressive*, February, 1976, p. 12.

pp. 114-115: Discussion of the size of nuclear bombs is based on The Boston Study Group, *The Price of Defense* (New York: Times Books, 1979), pp. 63-64. The definiton of "rem" is from Webster's Unabridged Dictionary.

pp. 115-116: The discussion, "An H-Bomb in Manhattan," is based on Tom Stonier, "What Would It Really Be Like? An H-Bomb on New York City," in Thomas Merton (ed.), *Breakthrough to Peace* (Norfolk, Ct.: New Directions, 1962), p. 30.

p. 117: LaRocque quote is from Center for Defense Information, *Nuclear War Prevention Kit* (Washington, DC: Center for Defense Information, 1980), p. 3. Quote from Lord Mountbatten is from "On the Brink of the Final Abyss," *Defense Monitor*, Vol. IX, No. 4 (May 1980), p. 4. All quotes from Lord Mountbatten are from this essay. The definition of "absolute war" is from Parkinson, p. 1.

pp. 118-119: Three essays on nuclear pacifism will be found in National Interreligious Service Board for Conscientious Objectors, *Words of Conscience* (Washington, DC: NISBCO, 1980), pp. 123-134.

p. 119: For treatment of the effect of railroads on warfare, see B. H. Liddell Hart, *Strategy*, p. 143.

Chapter 11

p. 121: *Gillette v. U.S.*, cited above, contains a good discussion of the use of force and how it differs from war.

p. 127: B. H. Liddell Hart discusses the military effect of gas in *The Real War*, cited above. Gas casualties as compared to casualties caused by "conventional" weapons will be found in

Crutwell, p. 630 ff.

Chapter 12

The major sources for this chapter were: Alan Bullock, *Hitler, A Study in Tyranny* (New York: Harper Colphon Books, 1964); A. J. P. Taylor, *The Origins of the Second World War* (Greenwich, Ct.: Fawcett, 1961); Peter Calvocoressi and Guy Wint, *Total War: The Story of World War II* (New York: Pantheon Books, 1972); Laurence Lafore, *The End of Glory: An Interpretation of the Origins of World War II* (Philadelphia and New York: J. B. Lippincott, 1970); Ellen Switzer, *How Democracy Failed* (New York: Atheneum, 1975); John Lukacs, *The Last European War September 1939/December 1941* (Garden City, N.Y.: Anchor Press/Doubleday, 1976). These are cited below by author's name.

p. 130: Casualty figures are from Parkinson, p. 149.

p. 130: Concentration camp figures are estimates only, from Lucy S. Davidowicz, *The War Against the Jews, 1933-1945* (New York: Holt, Rinehart & Winston, 1975), p. 403, and Calvocoressi and Wint, p. 236.

pp. 130-131: The leading advocate of the "Hitler's war" theory is Alan Bullock. A. J. P. Taylor takes the contrary view.

p. 131: On the "German Problem" and the two world wars, see Lafore, p. 11, and Taylor, p. 22, 44.

p. 131: Calvocoressi and Wint, pp. 551-553, give a comparison of World War I and World War II casualty figures.

pp. 131-132: Taylor, pp. 27-32, outlines the provisions of the Treaty of Versailles. See also D. F. Fleming, *The Origins and Legacy of World War I* (Garden City, N.Y.: Doubleday, 1968), pp. 264-280.

p. 132: On *Freikorps*, see Calvocoressi and Wint, p. 30.

p. 132: Description of the German inflation is quoted from John Kenneth Galbraith, *Money: Whence It Came, Where It Went* (Boston: Houghton Mifflin, 1975), p. 156.

p. 132: Description of German unemployment is quoted from Switzer, p. 45.

p. 133: Nazi seats in the German parliament: figure quoted from Bullock, p. 169. Hitler's appointment as Chancellor from Bullock, pp. 248-250.

p. 133: Henry Ford's support of Hitler: see Lukacs, p. 252 fn. See also Albert Lee, *Henry Ford and the Jews* (New York: Stein and Day, 1981).

p. 133: Passage from Anne Morrow Lindbergh quoted in Switzer, pp. 153-154.

p. 134: British and French made Munich proposal: Taylor, pp. 146-181.

p 134: Popularity of "appeasement": Taylor, p. 292.

p. 135: British leaders supporting terms with Hitler: Calvocoressi and Wint, p. 50.

p. 136: Hitler declared war on U.S.: Calvocoressi and Wint, pp. 184-185.

p. 136: Aim of the *Blitzkrieg*: Calvocoressi and Wint, p. 117.

p. 136: Development of *Blitzkrieg* theory: Calvocoressi and Wint, p. 117.

p. 136: On the Battle of Cambrai, see Liddell Hart, *The Real War*, pp. 344-356.

p. 136: Casualties in Norway fighting: Lukacs, p. 242. Somme casualty figure from John Keegan, *The Face of Battle, op.cit.*, p. 255. Keegan's figure is the one now generally accepted by historians.

Quote on the effects of *Blitzkrieg*: Lukacs, pp. 242-243.

p. 137: Hitler's order to level Germany: Albert Speer, *Inside the Third Reich* (New York: MacMillan, 1970), p. 561-562.

p. 137: A history of the British part of the "area bombing" campaign will be found in Max Hastings, *Bomber Command* (New York: Dial Press, 1979).

p. 138: Quote on the effects of area bombing: Calvocoressi and Wint, p. 501.

pp. 138-139: On willingness of countries to accept emigrant German Jews: Calvocoressi and Wint, p. 238.

p. 139: Establishment of Dachau: Calvocoressi, p. 228.

p. 139: Quote on decision to exterminate the Jews: Davidowicz, p. 121.

p. 139: Quote on American apathy: Arthur D. Morse, *While Six Million Died* (New York: Random House, 1968), p. 383.

p. 140: On the Turkish massacres of Armenians, see Kerop Bedoukian, *Some of Us Survived: The Story of an Armenian Boy* (New York: Farrar, Straus, Giroux, 1978). Figures are quoted from p. 238 of this book.

Chapter 13

p. 145: On Napoleon's invasion of Russia, see R. F. Delderfield, *The Retreat From Moscow* (New York: Atheneum, 1967). Russia has been invaded by foreign forces three times since 1800. In addition to Napoleon's disastrous attempt, the Western Allies (Britain, France, and the U.S.) invaded Russian territory in 1919. See John Bradley, *Allied Intervention in Russia* (New York: Basic Books, 1968). And German troops invaded Soviet territory in World War II, leading to fighting which killed about 20 million. See Harrison Salisbury, *The Unknown War* (New York: Bantam, 1978).

p. 147: A good but frightening discussion of the so-called "Rapid Deployment Force," which would be used if the U.S. went to war for oil, is found in Michael T. Klare, "An Army in Search of a

War," *The Progressive*, Vol. 45, No. 2 (February 1981), pp. 18-23.
P. 148: Defense Department use of oil: *Defense Monitor*, Vol. VIII, No. 11 (December 1979), p. 7.

Chapter 14

p. 154: On "basis in fact": *Estep v. U.S.*, 327 US 114 (1946).

pp. 154-155: On "exhaustion of administrative remedies," see *Falbo v. U.S.*, 320 US 549 (1944); *McGee v. U.S.*, 402 US 479 (1971); *McKart v. U.S.*, 395 US 185 (1969); *Gibson v. U.S.*, 329 US 338 (1946); *U.S. v. Stephens*, 4 SSLR 3308 (3rd Cir. 1971).

p. 155: On injunctions against induction orders, see *Ostereich v. Selective Service System*, 393 US 233 (1968); *Breen v. Local Board*, 396 US 460 (1970); *Clark v. Gabriel*, 393 US 256 (1968).

p. 155: On CO and habeas corpus, see, e.g., *Scott v. Commanding Officer*, 431 F.2d 1132 (3rd Cir. 1971).

p. 167: On "basis in fact," see *Estep*, cited above, and *Dickinson v. U.S.*, 346 US 389 (1953).

p. 167: On errors of law: *U.S. v. Prescott*, 301 F.Supp. 1116 (D.N.H. 1969); *U.S. v. Haffner*, 301 F.Supp. 828 (D. Hawaii 1969).

p. 167: On the need for evidence: *Witmer v. U.S.*, 348 US 375 (1955); "It is well-settled," etc., quoted from *Bates v. Commander, First Coast Guard District*, 413 F.2d 475 (1st Cir. 1969); see also *U.S. v. James*, 417 F.2d 826 (4th Cir. 1969); *U.S. v. Hesse*, 417 F.2d 141 (8th Cir. 1969); *U.S. v. Martin*, 416 F.2d 44 (10th Cir. 1969). "The mere assertion," etc., quoted from *Peckat v. Lutz*, 4 SSLR 3759 (4th Cir. 1971).

p. 167: On procedural errors, see for example *U.S. v. Zieber*, 161 F.2d 90 (3rd Cir. 1947).

p. 167: New information not considered: *U.S. v. Smith*, 292 F.Supp. 63 (D.N.H. 1968).

p. 167: No chance to reply to negative evidence: *U.S. v. Fisher*, 442 F.2d 109 (7th Cir. 1971).

p. 168: Wrong information given to registrant: *U.S. v. Burns*, 431 F.2d 1070 (10th Cir. 1970).

p. 168: Failure to state reasons: *U.S. v. St. Clair*, 293 F.Supp. 337 (E.D.N.Y. 1968); *U.S. v. Broyles*, 423 F.2d 1299 (4th Cir. 1970) (*en banc*); *Clay v. U.S.*, 403 US 698 (1971).

p. 168: Illegal time limit on personal appearance: *U.S. v. Peebles*, 220 F.2d 114 (7th Cir. 1955).

p. 168: Illegal reopening of classification: *U.S. v. Pence*, 410 F.2d 557 (8th Cir. 1969).

p. 168: Illegal refusal to reopen classification: *Mulloy v. U.S.*, 398 US 410 (1970).

Chapter 15

This chapter was prepared in consultation with Prisoner Visitation and Support Committee.

Chapter 16

Sources for this chapter are cited in the text.

INDEX

absence without leave, 1
Afghan invasion, 4, 9, 96
Algerian War, 4
American Civil War, 104-105, 146
Armenian Massacres, 140
arms race—see war
artillery—see war
Auschwitz, 139

Bering Straits, 144
Brahms, Johannes, 140
Brazil, 140
Burundi, 140

Cambodia, 140
Cambrai, Battle of, 136
Canada, 144
Chamberlain, Neville, 134
China, 7
Cold War, 95, 96, 140
Congress, 5, 13, 20
conscientious objection, 2, 90
  1-0 classification, 61-62
  actions in support of claim, 75-76
  alternative service—see draft
  CCCO card, 75
  "deeply held" beliefs, 57-58
  documentation, 71-83
  in Greece, 2
  "late" claims, 60
  noncombatant (1-A-0), 61-62, 182-186
    Army Medical Service, 183-185
    discharge and transfer, 185-186
    training and duties, 182-183
  personal moral code, 58
  political beliefs, 59
  provision for COs, 53-54
  "religious" beliefs, 2, 53-54
  religious training, 56-57
  selective objection—see selective objection
  sincerity, 59-60
  showing a history, 73-74
  supporting evidence, 72-73
  supporting letters, 76-77
  use of force, 64-65—see also force
  war in any form, 57, 63-65—see also selective objection
  writing claim, 78-82
conscription—see draft
court procedures
  arraignment, 163-164
  appeal, 169
  arrest, 160-161
  criminal prosecution, 156-157
  defenses, 167-168
  entering a plea, 164-165
  FBI investigation, 159
  judicial review, 154-156
  jurisdiction, 157-158
  preliminary hearing and indictment, 159-160
  pre-sentence investigation, 168
  release on bond, 161-163
  repeated prosecutions, 169-170
  sentencing, 168-169
  trial 165-166
courts, 5, 153-170
Cuba, 144
Cuban Missile Crisis, 146

Dachau, 139
defense budget, 7-8
Defense Department, 7, 13
  use of oil, 148
DeGaulle, Charles, 136
deterrence, 8, 117-118
Dien Bien Phu, Siege of, 96
draft, 1, 3, 7
  aliens and 28, 41
  alternative service, 36-37, 85-90
  appeal boards, 20
  appeals, 32-33
  armed forces physical, 18
  in Britain, 63, 87
  classification, 24-29
  induction authority, 18
  inductions, 18, 24, 35-36
  law, 18
    quoted, 53-54
  local boards, 20
  lottery, 21-23
  and military intervention, 14
  and military strategy, 14
  noncombatant service, 36-37
    —see also conscientious objection
  order of call, 23-24
  personal appearance, 30-32
  procedures, 18-37
  reasons for denying claims, 33-34
  and recruitment, 12
  registration, 13, 20-21, 41-52
  regulations, 18
  rights of registrants, 29-30
  standby, 13
  structure, 18-20
  Uniform National Call, 22-23
  violations and penalties, 49
draft resistance, 45-49, 51-52
  statements for court, 82-83
Dresden, 138

Europe, 7, 9, 13

Fay, Sidney B., 110, 112
Federal Emergency Management Agency, 86-87

force
  definition, 121-122
  military force, 8, 126-127
  police force, 125-126
  revolutionary, 123-125
  self-defense, 121, 122-123
  and violence, 122
Ford, Henry, 133
Franco-Prussian War, 105
Freikorps—see Germany
French Revolution, 123, 124
Fromm, Erich, 137
Fuller, J. F. C., 136

"geopolitics," 8, 96
"German problem," 131, 140
Germany
  depression, 132-133
  Freikorps, 132
  inflation, 132
  war reparations, 131, 132
Greece, 2
guerilla warfare—see war

Hiroshima, 113
Hitler, Adolf, 129-141, 143
  death camps, 130
  destructiveness, 137
  in 1930s, 133
Holocaust, 135, 138-140

Iran, 148
Iran-Iraq War, 96

Jehovah's Witnesses, 153

Korean War, 4, 9, 96, 146

LaRocque, Gene, 117, 118
lawyers, 158-159
League of Nations, 131, 135
Liddell Hart, B. H., 136, 138
Lindbergh, Anne Morrow, 133

Martel, G. LeQ., 136
Maximilianus, 1
Mexico, 144
Miami, 123, 124
militarism, 110-111

military force—see force
Mountbatten, Lord, 117, 118, 120

Napoleon, 106
    and conscription, 14
    invasion of Russia, 145
NATO, 9
nuclear pacifism, 118-119
nuclear war
    deterrence—see deterrence
    effects, 113-114, 115-116
    limited, 119-120
    size of bombs, 114-115
    strategy, 116-118
    "tactical" weapons, 119-120
    weapons, 7

"pacification," 126
Peace Pledge campaign, 148-149
Pearl Harbor, 143-144
Pentagon—see Defense Department
"Pentagonese," 103
Persian Gulf, 96
poison gas—see war
President, 18
prisons, 171-177
    county jail, 172-173
    federal prison, 173-174
    prison life, 174-177
Prisoner Visitation and Support, 178
Proudhon, Pierre Joseph, 124

racism, 4
Reign of Terror, 124
"religious" beliefs—see conscientious objection
Riegner, Gerhart, 139
Russian Revolution, 123, 124

selective objection
    defined, 64-65
    Just War Theory, 66-68
    just war objectors, 67-68
    supporters, 69
Sherman, William Tecumseh, 105

Sherman's March to the Sea, 105, 126-127
"shortfall," 11-12
Siege of Paris, 105
Somme, Battle of, 136
Soviet Union—see USSR
Stalin, Josef, 124
Supreme Court, 125
Sweden, 148

Third World, 4, 9, 10
Treaty of Versailles, 131-132

Uganda, 140
unemployment, 4, 10
USSR, 4, 7, 8
    invasion of U.S., 144-145
United States, 4, 8
    attack on, 143-150
        and fear, 150
        and patriotism, 149-150
        vital interests, 147-148
        unprovoked, 145-146
United States military, 7, 8
    recruitment, 10-12

Verdun, Battle of 96, 104, 109
Vietnam War, 4, 9, 14, 96, 106, 126, 146, 149
    officer casualties, 99
violence—see force

war, 1, 95-112
    and arms race, 97-98
    artillery, 10, 107, 127
    "of attrition," 14
    casualties, 113
    causes, 111-112
    combat, 107-109
    costs, 109-110
    counter insurgency, 106
    definition, 95-97
    guerilla, 10, 106
    language of, 103-104
    laws of, 102-103, 127
    military structure, 98-100
    modern, 67-68, 119
    nuclear—see nuclear war
    poison gas, 102, 127

and racism, 4, 11
and railroads, 104-105
total, 104-105
trench warfare, 137
weapons of, 100-101
and women, 4, 11
war crimes, 125
War Department, 7
war resisters, 1, 2
war resistance, 2-3
civil disobedience, 50
tax resistance, 50
Warsaw Pact, 9, 13
Waterloo, Battle of, 96
Watts, 124
weapons systems, 9
women—see war
World War I, 14, 95, 96, 119, 131
casualties, 113, 131, 136
draft, 153
officer casualties, 100
weapons, 98
World War II, 4, 95-96, 109, 110, 146
appeasement, 134
"area bombing," 137
Blitzkrieg, 130-136-137
casualties, 130, 131, 135
draft, 153
Norway fighting, 136
Nuremberg Trials, 125
origins, 130-136
Siege of Leningrad, 130

LIST OF CASES CITED

Bates v. Commander, First Coast Guard District, 60, 167
U.S. v. Berg, 67
Breen v. Local Board, 155
U.S. v. Broyles, 168
U.S. v. Burns, 168

U.S. v. Carson, 61
Clark v. Gabriel, 155
Clay v. U.S., 54, 168
Dickinson v. U.S., 167

Estep v. U.S., 154, 167

Falbo v. U.S., 154-155
U.S. v. Fisher, 167
Fleming v. U.S., 59

Gibson v. U.S., 154-155
Gillette v. U.S., 57, 64, 121

U.S. v. Haffner, 167
In re Hansen, 56
U.S. v. Hesse, 60, 167

U.S. v. James, 60, 167

Kemp v. Bradley, 58

McGee v. U.S., 154-155
McKart v. U.S., 154-155
U.S. v. Martin, 60, 167
Mulloy v. U.S., 168

In re Nissen, 56

Ostereich v. Selective Service System, 155
U.S. v. Owen, 64

Peckat v. Lutz, 167
U.S. v. Peebles, 168
U.S. v. Pence, 168
U.S. v. Prescott, 167
U.S. v. Purvis, 57

U.S. v. Relyea, 61

U.S. v. St. Clair, 168
Scott v. Commanding Officer, 155
U.S. v. Seeger, 55-56, 59
Sicurella v. U.S., 57
U.S. v. Smith, 167
U.S. v. Stephens, 154-155
U.S. v. Stewart, 65

Welsh v. U.S., 55-56, 59
U.S. v. Willson, 65
Witmer v. U.S., 167

U.S. v. Zieber, 167

The Author

Robert A. Seeley joined the CCCO staff in 1968. From then until 1972, he was a draft counselor. Since 1972 he has been Editor of *CCCO News Notes*, a military counselor, and CCCO publications coordinator. His articles on conscientious objection, the draft, and war resistance have been published in *The Progressive*, the *Friends Journal*, and *Confrontation*, among other places.